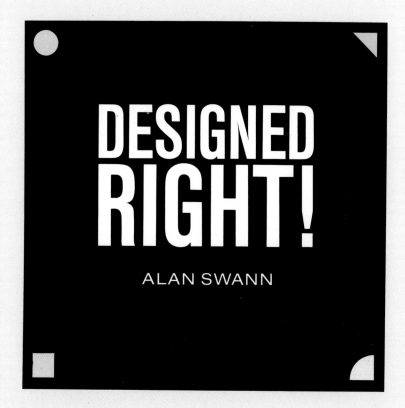

DESIGNED RIGHT!

ALAN SWANN

DESIGNED RIGHT!

ALAN SWANN

NORTH LIGHT BOOKS

Cincinnati, Ohio

A QUARTO BOOK

First published in the U.S.A. by
North Light Books, an imprint of
F & W Publications, Inc
1507 Dana Avenue
Cincinnati, Ohio 45207

This book was designed and produced by
Quarto Publishing plc
The Old Brewery, 6 Blundell Street
London N7 9BH

Senior Editor Susanna Clarke
Editor Richard Dawes

Design Alan Swann
Picture Research Sheila Geraghty
Illustrators David Kemp, John Scorey
Photographer Martin Norris

Art Director Moira Clinch
Assistant Art Director Chloë Alexander
Editorial Director Carolyn King

Special thanks go to Mervyn Kurlansky, Glen Tutssel, Amelia Gatacre,
Deborah Hale, Paul Diner, Mike Tapson and K. Patel.

Typeset by Ampersand Typesetting Limited, Bournemouth
Manufactured in Hong Kong by
Regent Publishing Services Limited
Printed in Hong Kong

CONTENTS

INTRODUCTION
6

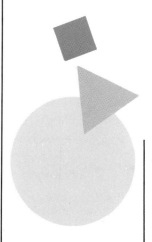

Introduction

THE ULTIMATE PURPOSE of a piece of graphic design is the visual message it communicates. The effectiveness of this message depends upon the right choice of graphic elements and their combination in a well-planned format. To communicate well the designer must have at his disposal a wide range of visual styles, either visualizing them from memory or using reference material. It is important for the designer to look at some of the historical influences that established distinctive styles within their periods. Today we see such styles as typical of their time, although we are also aware that, if used badly, they can appear clichéd. It is not enough just to look at one or two references when researching a graphic style to convey a particular period. In fact, the most original designs are found by taking the trouble to seek out less obvious pieces of work.

No hard-and-fast rules govern the creation of graphic styles or images, yet there are nevertheless conventions that make the work of the designer easier and help us to understand the effect he wishes to create. The composer of music follows (and breaks) conventions in combining notes to form melodies and harmonies. Similarly, in the field of graphic communication the designer follows established guidelines in combining elements such as color, tone, type, illustration and photographs. These graphic elements are assembled in a controlled and deliberate manner in order to stimulate the viewer. The effects are as varied as those of music, ranging from the visual equivalent of a sophisticated symphony to that of the drive and immediacy of rock 'n' roll.

By following different visual conventions when combining design elements, the designer can communicate different messages. But to give each message a style that is both distinctive and works, it is necessary to choose the right elements. These have been evolved over centuries by sensitive and dedicated artists and designers. For example, typefaces continue to proliferate, serving changing tastes and styles within society. Their contribution to the style of a piece of work is often paramount to its success. Color, borders and illustrations are also key factors in the styling of a piece of graphic design.

But more important to the designer than the

individual elements is the design brief, for this dictates the use that is made of them. The brief is normally generated and managed by the client, who will often engage the services of market researchers to help determine the audience at which the design is to be aimed and the style which is most likely to engage their attention. For example, a natural product such as bread may be marketed in a way that sparks off in the potential consumer a set of visual associations such as sunsets, sheaves of corn, country life and earthy colors. These associations will help in establishing the nature of the product. This is a simple example, most graphic design projects are not so straightforward, requiring greater insight and more inventiveness to achieve the goal set by the brief.

This book is an in-depth study of the elements of design and their use in formulating a wide range of graphic styles. It begins by examining each element in detail, allowing you to build up a visual library that will be instrumental in making the correct design decision. For example, by adding the right type at the right size and printing it in the right color, with perhaps a further ingredient such as an illustra-tion or photograph, you will be able to construct an effective and appropriate piece of graphic design.

The next section of the book explains how to create a style suitable for a specific market, and how design elements can be combined in different ways to achieve a variety of styles. It shows what is meant by traditional or classic style; how a retrospective style is created; how a style can be targeted at a young market; and how mass-market appeal is generated through exciting graphic displays.

The final section presents the work in progress of a selection of experienced graphic designers from various fields. A series of documentary photographs enables you to understand the creative decisions made by today's top designers as they style the images that will surround us in the future.

Armed with this book, you will have a deeper insight into successful graphic communication style and will be able to make clearer and more positive graphic decisions, whether you are creating the brief or creating the work itself.

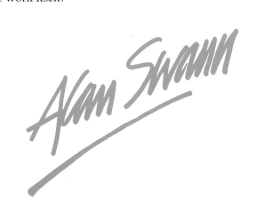

WHAT IS STYLE?

TO IMPROVE YOUR ability to understand and apply graphic styles, you must first realize that images have a language and communicative force. Style can be defined only in retrospect, and studying earlier designs allows you to appreciate landmarks in its evolution. In assessing past work you must consider every facet of the design and ask yourself a number of questions.

The first of these questions concerns the overall effect of the work, the feeling it conveys and who it is aimed at. A piece of work should describe the quality, atmosphere and message intended by the designer. The next area to investigate is the elements of the design, which themselves contribute to the style. The typeface is the most important of these and the easiest to define.

TYPEFACE STYLE

Typefaces have been created specifically to communicate different visual qualities and there are many safe choices that can be used to reflect your required style. Typefaces have evolved over centuries and you can depict established historical styles by referring to the distinctive types used at the time. However, innovative design often re-uses these typefaces in a different context to convey a personal style or interpretation.

COLOR, PHOTOGRAPHY AND ILLUSTRATION

Color has many qualities, from a simple directness to subtle symbolism. Age and established qualities can be conveyed by a judicious choice of single or mixed colors.

Photography and illustration can play an enormous role in styling graphic work, as their individuality and scope can dominate and control the visual effect of a design. The work of the photographer and illustrator is often selected for its compatibility with the style the designer is attempting to achieve.

The designer's role is to deploy the elements so as

to create a style that suits the client's brief. Each designer's own artistic approach leads him or her to define a visual language and use it to interpret the brief in a personal way.

EVOLVING STYLE

Although there are categories of style, they are by no means static and inflexible. Yesterday's forgotten styles can, with a fresh interpretation, become the high fashion of today.

The designer of styles for the mass market must be a step ahead of the public because design of this kind can quickly become boring and unattractive.

To create effective designs, the designer must absorb a wealth of visual information on which his or her imagination can feed. This requirement is as important in the ephemeral field of mass-market design as it is for the creation of lasting work.

Landmarks in Style

BEFORE THE TWENTIETH century the major influences on design came from fine art. Artists were often engaged to create publicity material based on their own distinctive style. In the last century, when publicity became a major industry, they embraced the newly available printing techniques.

The themes and sentiments of popular art were often reflected in the design styles of the day. But the images were modified to make them compatible with the print processes. Such modification led to styles that were in many cases unique to the period. Some of the masters of this new industry saw it as an opportunity to create images that appealed to a far wider audience than that reached by fine art, and to encourage a greater appreciation of the visual language. These artist-designers were themselves influenced both by the styles of the past and the fashions of their time.

The distinctive qualities of these pages from a 1920s catalogue have been achieved by using delicate border and scroll motifs surrounding a series of controlled and effective layouts created with highly detailed and realistic drawing and shaded backgrounds. The typography has the same degree of delicacy and is sympathetically chosen.

1 Dating from the 1880s, this label for Agua de Florida perfume imitates an earlier rival created by Rimmel. The designer recognized the success of the Rimmel design, and his astute choice of images has paid off, as the product is still available today in the same form.

1

2

3 The box is decorated with many interlocking graphic devices. Their complexity gives the design stability and permanence. The

3

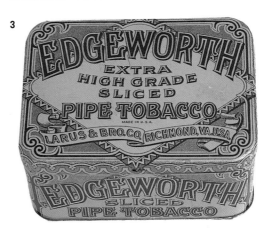

design lent a distinctive identity to this product that was reflected in the retail shops and their fascia designs.

4 This successful product was marketed with the same package design for 72 years. Its impact on design up to 1960 was so great that it influenced similar mass-market products.

4

2 Aubrey Beardsley's work for the publisher John Lane established a unique style that was used in the creation of fashionable graphics long after the artist's death. The subtle and limited use of color gives the impression of quality and high fashion.

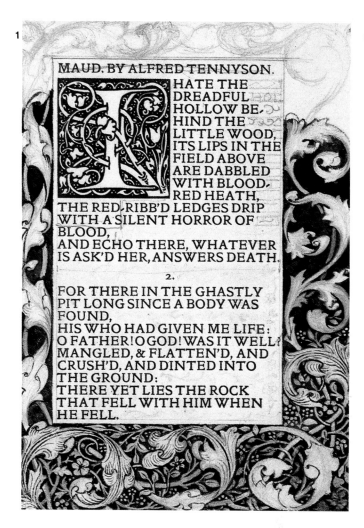

1 William Morris's distinctive style of design draws upon the images of an earlier period, blending them into decorative and romantic patterns. Morris's work inspired many designers, who used his geometrically constructed floral designs in numerous ways.

2 Peter Behrens's AEG logo design of around 1907 was the inspiration for a new movement in functional design.

VICTORIAN STYLE

At the end of the nineteenth century William Morris had a major influence on English design. His knowledge of and sympathy with medieval and classical images appealed to the Victorian taste for decorative styles, and his use of linear, floral images intertwined into complex patterns formed the basis of much late-Victorian imagery. Illustrators such as Aubrey Beardsley and Will Bradley gave illustration a new styling that exploited simple outline patterns. These were suited to the methods of printing and the bold designs to be found on many Victorian products.

Graphic design of this time was often styled to reflect brand qualities, nationalities and far-off, exotic countries where luxury products or their ingredients originated. The images used to promote luxury products were often both visually complex and wordy. In many cases such designs faced no competition from other brands, so the styling had only to appeal to a small number of consumers who had clearly defined lifestyles that were in turn reflected in these images. More mundane items, such as cleaning products, were embellished with simple but eye-catching graphics, which is still the formula employed for promoting most mass-market products today.

BEGINNINGS OF MODERN STYLE

Early in the present century, designers revolted against the flowery nature of late-nineteenth-century graphics and adopted a more functional approach that reflected the power and increased productivity of modern industry. Peter Behrens transformed the graphic styling of AEG in Germany in 1907 with his simplified corporate identity that brought together several modern graphic design elements into a single design. This piece of work inspired a new European movement in which design no longer relied on traditional images but invented its own to reflect the qualities of a new range of products and lifestyles.

These images, some quite abstract in nature, developed in parallel with more conventional visual ideas. The work of Behrens and his like-minded contemporaries freed the designer to cross visual boundaries and to control imagery and styling with a mobility that had until then been the sole preserve of artists.

3 A. M. Cassandre's approach to design took shapes from life and molded them into a style that set the tone for the late 1920s. His experimentation extended from illustration to typography, in which each element was manipulated to gain maximum impact in communicating to a mass audience.

4 By the 1930s, Lever Brothers were selling this famous product in 134 countries, helped no doubt by its commercial branding. The design with its bold product name accommodated panels for information in local languages.

1 E. McKnight-Kauffer created a style with simple geometric elements, carefully divided space and inventive use of color and type. The images are simple, belying the complex structure of the design, which still appears sophisticated today. His work was also well suited to the ever-changing methods of print production.

2 This highly stylized package design of the 1920s illustrates the practice of borrowing styles from other countries and molding them to suit a mass audience.

3 Ludwig Hohlwein's pioneering style of illustration and hand-drawn type had a mass appeal in Germany between the world wars. His work was featured on pack designs and on many mass-produced commercial products.

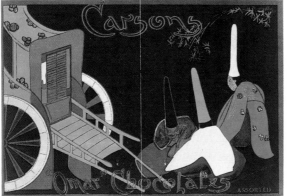

As consumerism developed and personal purchasing power increased, the markets became more fragmented, demanding greater individuality in all areas of design. Products required a style of presentation that reinforced their appeal to a specific audience.

STYLE AND MARKET

Today, we can re-use such visual information to create new designs. In addition, current design skills and the scientific formulae used to produce designs make it possible to convey a specific visual message.

The style of the design is of paramount importance to the message it conveys, since consumers are conscious of the images they relate to and wish to relate to. Imagery and styling for the youth market, for example, must be in tune with the particular characteristics of this group. Furthermore, the structure of modern society is complex, and people from different backgrounds respond differently to visual styles. Today's designer must therefore not only be familiar with both historical and contemporary references, but also be aware of the complex nature of modern society.

4 This highly pictorial design has been underpinned with carefully conceived graphic elements. This style of design is still imitated today wherever detailed illustration is required.

5 Throughout this century designers have been influenced by the work of innovative artists. El Lissitzky was one of the greatest influences, and echoes of his work still appear today.

1

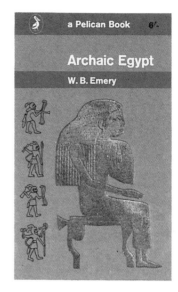

The Stagnant Society — a Pelican Book 3/6 — Michael Shanks

The Managerial Revolution — a Pelican Book 4/- — James Burnham

A Short History of French Literature — a Pelican Book 5/- — Geoffrey Brereton

Archaic Egypt — a Pelican Book 6/- — W. B. Emery

1 The early 1960s saw a change in all areas of graphic design, led by new avant-garde designers such as Germano Facetti, Colin Forbes and Ole Vedel. These book covers commissioned by Penguin marked the emergence of a new and exciting design style.

2 This pack for an Olivetti typewriter was designed by Alan Fletcher. The designer has played on the idea of the typewriter ribbon in the creation of the ribbon-like typography.

2

3 Distinctive styles of the past can be recreated in modern contexts, reaffirming their value and communicating a new message to a new audience. This design by Alan Fletcher acknowledges the inspiration of A. M. Cassandre's famous advertisement for Dubonnet of 1933.

3

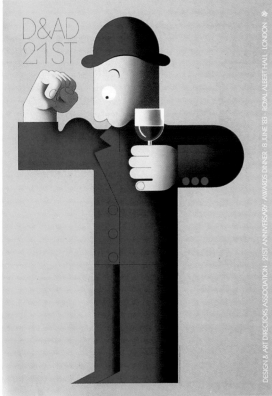

4 This poster, from a set of 26 representing the alphabet, promotes a photosetting firm. A new poster became available every two weeks for one year and the recipient was able to make initials or spell words to be hung on the wall. The set of posters was silk-screen printed using a six color palette.

5 From the late 1960s Habitat styling started a new trend in British mass-market catalogue design. The company's international presence influenced graphic design in many countries.

6 Graphic design as a direct means of communicating an educational message is illustrated particularly well by this work created by Colin Forbes in 1966.

6

5

4

CHECKLIST

- Seek the most influential designs of the period that interests you.
- Analyze their audience.
- Distinguish between different periods in design history.
- Study each of the elements closely and assess their visual value.
- Build up a collection of design references.

THE ELEMENTS OF STYLE

THE CREATION OF style in graphic design relies on many elements, each with a broad visual scope. This part of the book examines the visual messages conveyed by the use of different graphic elements. One of the most difficult tasks is to make the right choice of elements and then mold them into a unified design solution. Although there is no definitive approach to the creation of style, there exist proven formulae that can be applied to establish a mood in a piece of work.

PUTTING ELEMENTS TOGETHER

It is important to understand the exact nature and visual messages of the elements within a design. Many designs miss their target, not because the individual elements have not been well thought out, but because their use together has not been considered carefully enough. The balance between the elements in a design is of prime importance in achieving a style. Nor is it possible to create an effective design by arranging your chosen elements in a single way. It is necessary to try out various permutations before you can make the final decision. The design should reflect the individuality of the designer. In the hands of a skilled designer, the elements can be combined to produce a result that could not have been predicted.

AN OBJECTIVE VIEW OF DESIGN

This part of the book, by increasing your visual repertoire, will give you greater control over your work. But you must also use this knowledge to develop an objective and realistic view of it. If you feel that one of your designs fails, analyze what it is that displeases you and adapt the design accordingly.

Shape, Size and Format

■ What constraints does the design brief impose on the shape?

■ Does the budget allow freedom in the choice of shape?

■ What images do you want your shape to conjure up?

■ Does your design require a unique shape?

■ Experiment with various shapes by drawing them.

■ Cut out shapes to evaluate their effect.

THE FIRST ELEMENTS to consider in any design are its shape, its format and its proportions. Shape is a distinctive contributing factor to the overall style, and, once you are aware of its potency, you will see everywhere examples of its inventive handling.

THE POSSIBILITIES

Shape can convey a wide range of qualities, from simplicity to sophistication, from conformity to uniqueness. In addition, the size at which it is used can give emphasis or create subtle appeal. In some cases the brief will determine the shape and size of your design, an obvious example being a standard display poster. In such cases the challenge is to exploit the format to the full while creating a style that is fitting to the message.

Shapes need not be unique or even unusual. Subtlety can be derived simply from the carefully considered use of a square or rectangle. Whatever the shape that you select, it should complement the overall style and the underlying design idea. Look at shapes used for other designs and consider their effectiveness in supporting the work.

WITHIN THE CHOSEN SHAPE

Once you have established your design's size, shape and proportions, decide on the angles at which the elements will be placed within this format. If the design is for a leaflet or booklet, there is the further question of how the shape opens up. Such considerations become more complex when the shape you are creating is for a three-dimensional design. In the case of packaging, the method of production should be considered in detail before you decide on a final shape, since your solution could be prohibitively expensive or difficult to manufacture.

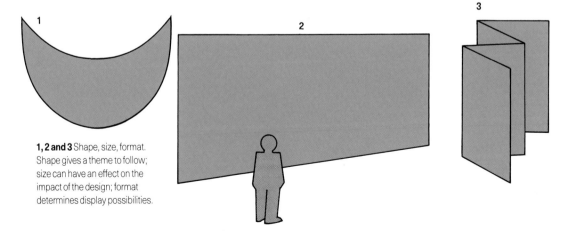

1, 2 and 3 Shape, size, format. Shape gives a theme to follow; size can have an effect on the impact of the design; format determines display possibilities.

4 A selection of shapes, sizes and proportional arrangements – just a few of the many possibilities to consider before applying graphic information to the surface.

Type and Style: Traditional

1 Letterforms together make a pattern that will assist in the styling. Variations in their spacing and the use of capitals or lower-case letters project different sorts of image. Changing the size of the letters within the design space also serves this purpose.

A MAJOR ELEMENT in any design is the typeface, which serves many purposes. Since the type style is the first element with which the viewer will identify, its selection should precede other considerations.

ADVANTAGES OF THE TRADITIONAL

Certain typefaces have become established for their combination of consistency and adaptability. Most of these traditional typefaces offer the designer a wide variety of visual choices, from bold, extended faces to light, condensed faces. What defines a typeface as traditional is its readability and acceptability when used in a conventional manner. Many of the traditional Roman typefaces, with their elegant serif forms, have become the cornerstones of conventional typography.

SANS-SERIF FACES

Some sans-serif faces have also become traditional in appeal. These have emerged mostly this century and several are now commonly used. The most widely used sans-serif typefaces offer a broad visual choice, allowing the designer to use compatible display type and body matter. If the combination of different sizes of typeface is to convey a traditional feel, the visual effect must be harmonious. However, not every type design enables such harmony to be achieved.

A limited number of faces possess a strictly traditional appeal. The designer's task is to challenge the conventions and attempt to break new typographic ground with innovative experimentation.

Traditional

TRADITIONAL

TRADITIONAL

Traditional Traditional

TRADITIONAL TRADITIONAL

TRADITIONAL

TRADITIONAL

2

 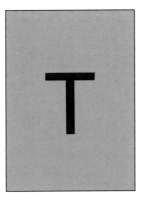 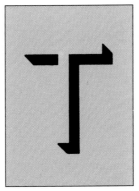 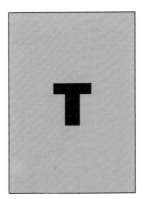

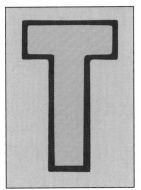   

2 By isolating a single letter, it is possible to concentrate on the typeface and style it projects. This exercise will make design decisions easier. The various visual possibilities of letterforms can also be assessed by experimentation.

3

3 This pack relies on color to set a traditional theme. It features an elegant use of blue and black, punctuated by the minimal use of red, which links the brand name to the product. The careful mix of typefaces, with serif and sans-serif complementing one another, is spaced to create a graceful central block. The illustration of Pulteney Bridge, in Bath, England, is used to symbolize the architecture of the English Regency period.

Type and Style: Modern

CHECKLIST
- ■ Seek out the typefaces that reflect certain periods.
- ■ Analyze the image they convey.
- ■ Check their availability in modern type books.
- ■ Compare them with other typefaces with a similar style.
- ■ Investigate new typefaces.
- ■ Familiarize yourself with the styling variations made possible by a computer.

SINCE THE BIRTH of the type industry, new typefaces have been generated in an attempt to stay ahead of changes in fashion. Each decade can be pinpointed by the distinctive and sometimes extravagant styles of its type design. Often these typefaces echo a sense of the art and technology of their time. They are useful to the modern designer who wants to establish a style that reflects a period or conveys a sense of the fashion of that era. They can also give the design a distinctive and exclusive appeal. When the designer's task is to create a style that suits a product or service, it may be necessary to opt for a typeface of the past and apply it in a new and modern context.

MANIPULATING TYPEFACES

At the same time, the proliferation of new typefaces is as great today as it has ever been, and with new technology and the opportunity to modify almost any typeface with a computer, there is further scope for the designer to create individually crafted styles of work. This potential is very apparent in work aimed at the youth market, and especially in stylish magazines. Even the traditional typefaces can be visually manipulated to forge new and exciting communication styles.

ADAPTING OLDER STYLES

An investigation of how typefaces were originally applied can show you how best to use them in a modern context. You will find that most modern faces are adaptations of historical sources and you will also discover that the styles of particular periods are sooner or later reworked. For example, the current interest in 1950s fashion has brought about the re-use and adaptation of typefaces characteristic of that period.

1

1 Modern typography tends to be distinguished by the way in which the typefaces are applied more than by anything else. Many faces, however, have been created recently, and with new technology it is also possible to experiment with traditional forms, giving them a new look by subtle modification.

2 The type image should always be considered for its illustrative power. Applied imaginatively, letterforms can often say more than a photograph or picture. In this colorful layout, typography has been used inventively, with a lively, modern sensitivity.

2

Type and Style: Distinctive

TO ACHIEVE A style suitable for a particular job, it is sometimes essential to ignore typefaces that are readily available, and seek out one that gives the work a distinctive and individual style.

Throughout the world there are typographic designers who are specialists in type development and the design of new typefaces. Because of their individual style, they are often commissioned to create new and unique images. But it is possible for most designers to adapt typefaces to accommodate special typographic needs. For example, typefaces are often specially created for a company logo or corporate identity.

ILLUSTRATIVE TYPE IMAGES

Letterforms can be developed into highly illustrative and colorful images. This form of type is closer to illustration and can be designed to project a specific and distinctive look. When you are creating new letterforms, it is important to base them on a well-chosen and readily available typeface. This will help you to grasp their flow and proportions. Remember, whatever new forms of type you create, they must be legible and adhere to the overall style you have set.

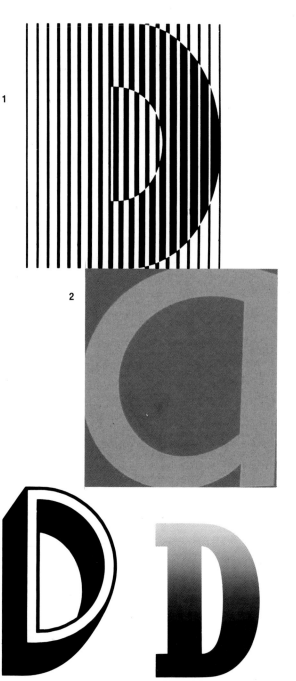

1 Existing letterforms can provide a basis for further development. By embellishing the image sympathetically, it is possible to lend it a personalized style.

2 The inventive manipulation of the type image can produce a wide variety of solutions to the task of appealing to a specific market. Color can be varied to bring elements of the design into prominence.

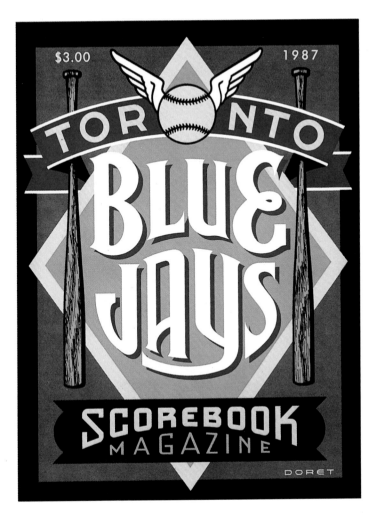

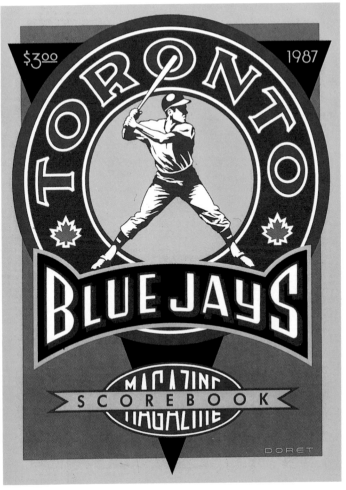

3 Isolating a design element allows you to assess its individual value and the part it plays in the overall design.

Formulae for Design Style: Borders and Decoration

IN THE NINETEENTH century most printed designs were contained within decorative calligraphic and illustrative borders, with scroll-work and pen decoration around and between the lines of type. Gradually, however, this form of decoration fell out of favor. By the 1920s, complicated decoration had disappeared, and the emphasis was on simple embellishment.

BORDERS

Borders, which can range from simple box rules to highly complex textile images, can set the basic theme for the style the project requires. In fact, a carefully chosen border can depict a period, convey quality and address a specific target audience.

Where there is only type to be displayed and this needs visual support to establish the style, a border can lend the design a distinctive character. The use of devices for dividing the design area can be problematic when the design is complex. In such cases you may wish to use devices with shapes that form a balance as a means of controlling the information to be displayed. By studying the shapes used in past and contemporary designs, you will discover solutions that you can use in your own.

1 With the right choice of border, it is possible to give your design an appropriate period feel. Tints and colors can be used to increase or lessen the importance of this mood.

1

2 Decorative borders and elements can be applied to letterforms, giving them a styling that evokes a period or is distinctly individual. Standard letterforms are available from graphics dealers and typesetters. Colors or the use of carefully selected tints can help you model a design to the appropriate style.

3

4

3 Borders can be used to contain the design, providing a shape or formula for other elements to follow. Colors can be added to create a visual pattern or to suggest a period.

4 Shapes can be placed within shapes or borders, and accompanied by images that explode out of the formal area, creating a dynamic or background feature.

1 Graphic devices should be assessed in terms of the style they impose on the overall design. By modeling your device on a period or on a trend, you can establish the right style for the work.

SHAPES

Another common device is oval shapes inside ovals or squares and circles inside each other. These can be distinctively set apart from one another or subtly harmonized with either a bold or a sensitive choice of colors.

THE POSSIBILITIES

Decorative design supports can simply echo the shape and format of the design or can be allowed to dominate it by covering its entire surface. Just by changing the proportions, color and length of a single line, you will begin to appreciate how the simplest of elements can be an effective tool. At the other extreme, a complex and decorative gilt-frame effect, possibly printed in a sympathetic color, can

lend authority to the overall design. Even embellishing a controlled column of text with a block, shape or decorative letterform will change the feeling entirely of the lace-like quality of the type.

CHOICE OF COLOR

Your choice of color for the borders and decorations can impart a particular quality to the design. Old-fashioned colored borders can be re-used in a modern context, and modern borders can be modified to convey age and other qualities. Even when only black is available, if you soften the image by reducing it to a tint, you can convey the merest hint of a presence. Alternatively, you can use black at full strength for impact.

2

2 Borders can be constructed from the simplest or the most complex forms. The mesh effect on these jackets gives continuity, while the color provides individuality.

3

3 A combination of borders and decals can be integrated into a single design to establish a theme and a market position.

4

4 A single enlarged border or element can become a central focus of a design. In this calendar the ethereal quality of the decoration is heightened by the gold.

CHECKLIST
- Investigate borders and decorative devices used in the past.
- Analyze how they can be of use in modern styling.
- Use colors and tints to vary the effect.
- Vary the proportions of these elements to change the emphasis.
- Experiment with visual alternatives and compare the effects.

Color in Style: Single Color

THE COLORS USED to establish the required mood or image for a design must be chosen with great care. Their suggestive powers play a profound role in communicating the right message. If they are wrongly applied, this sensitive design ingredient will forcibly detract from the original intention. Each color you choose must be suitable for the design.

When a single color is used, its power and the extent to which it is applied must be experimented with before a decision is made. Single printed colors can be specified at the printing stage, when your chosen color can be mixed. When your choice is restricted, it is often wise to choose a passive color, since the vibrancy of bright natural color can often distract the viewer's attention from the message and style the piece is attempting to convey. However, the appropriate and controlled use of a single bright color can in some cases work in favor of the product or service advertised.

CONVEYING AGE AND QUALITY

The use of a single dark shade of green, blue or red can give the impression of age, and such colors are often used to convey the notion of established quality and sophistication.

Explore also the variety of shades that can be extracted from a single color. By reducing a solid area of color to various tints of the original, it is possible to create a sense of depth and to modify the overall style. The tints themselves can be adjusted to change the color effect, and you can use coarse tints or fine meshes of any density.

1 The use of white out of a pastel tint creates a delicate effect.

2 Warm colors can be thinned by reducing the density of the tint to create soft, comfortable effects.

3 Choose color both for its appropriateness to the design and also for its strength. Forceful colors such as yellow stand out from surrounding tones.

4 Various screens can be applied to give the color harmonious textures that enhance the overall impact of a design.

5 Darker colors can give authority to a design and provide scope for creating a broad range of graduated tints.

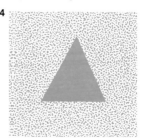

6 The Open College of the Arts · Houndhill · Worsbrough · Barnsley · South Yorkshire S70 6TU

An Exhibition of Work by

Students on the Foundation,

Painting, Sculpture and

Textiles Courses

at the Central School (Central
Saint Martins College of Art & Design)
Southampton Row, London WCI.

FROM JULY 18-21, 1989

THE EXHIBITION IS OPEN FROM 10 AM TO 4 PM

6 This poster has been printed in a single color, blue. The headline logo has been given emphasis by applying tints within the outline letter shapes. The illustration makes use of an enlarged newsprint screen to create areas with an interesting uneven tone to contrast well with the line drawing of the head.

7 These product containers have been colored with pastel shades, to give minimal color but the maximum impression of delicacy and sensitivity.

8 The solid blue used to contain the white-out design exemplifies sophisticated and confident styling.

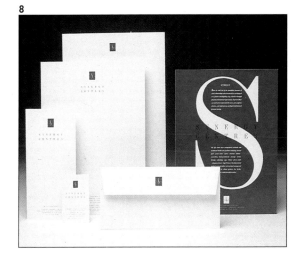

Color in Style: Full Color

THE USE OF full color offers the designer limitless scope, particularly since modern printing techniques make it possible to capture any nuance of style. However, the restrained use of color is often more effective than a complex arrangement of several colors.

Colors can be used to set the overall mood of your design. They can give it a realistic three-dimensional appeal by revealing texture and form, or can suggest the past or even totally imaginary worlds. The use of patterns is another way of exploiting the availability of different colors. Flat colors can be used to cover background areas or, as cut-out shapes, they can support the main elements of the design. From the primary source, colors can be mixed to give a unique look to a piece of work.

SYMBOLIC USE OF COLOR

Periods of history, national characteristics, seasons of the year, and emotions can all be evoked or symbolized by the use of color.

Full color is used to its best advantage when color photographs and illustrations are incorporated in the design.

1 This logo was designed for Cannon Babysafe, for an international market. The product is rooted in advanced technology, and the bright, primary colors used on the packaging stand out and can be identified among crowded displays. The typeface is inspired by the alphabet designed by Cassandre.

1

2

2 This design for the Channel Tunnel uses full-color printing to produce a rich combination of the colors which are associated with concern for the environment.

The background colors used on this page – cyan on the folio strips, yellow over page 34 and magenta over page 35 – are the basic colors used to print full-color work. Most colors in printed work are derived from these three primaries, and black and the white surface of the paper are used to strengthen or lighten the mix of colors.

Zwei Rätsel von Seymour Chwast:
links ein Labyrinth,
rechts ein Suchbild:
wieviele Dinge sind falsch?

3 Here a colorful image has been made by using flat colors of a brand-name ink system. Six colors were carefully chosen and incorporated within the design. The effect is richly bright and almost kaleidoscopic.

Color in Style: Special Effects

CHECKLIST
■ Investigate the special effects that can be produced in color.

■ Study examples of work that use metallic finishes.

■ See how the iridescent colors assist in the styling process.

■ Analyze their qualities.

■ Build up a library of special colors used to create style.

TO ACHIEVE A desired style, you may need to introduce a special color. For example, gold and silver are often printed into a design. They can be used to great effect when the notion of quality needs to be conveyed. Many champagne labels, for example, include simulated precious-metal finishes. However, there is a fine line between suggesting quality and creating a cheap, "glitzy" effect, so caution must be used when applying metallic colors.

Iridescent colors can be used to create striking designs. But, again, caution is needed, since the rawness of these colors can destroy the overall style if they are applied inappropriately.

PRINTING REQUIREMENTS

Special colors can be printed separately from the full-color process. For example, when a particular solid color is required, say, for a background into which full-color illustrations are to be inserted, it may be necessary to print the background as a separate print run. When it comes to the final print, a design often calls for extra colors to achieve the precise effect specified on the initial design.

PRINTING TECHNIQUES

The different color-printing processes produce different results. There is, for example, a great difference in quality and appeal between litho and silkscreen printing. Even the old letterpress process can be exploited to create a particular style. Investigate the different printing techniques and seek advice from your printer, who will be able to show you samples of the best use of each. Also, by studying a wide range of readily available printed material, you will be able to identify where colors have been printed to achieve special effects.

1 In this illustration two complementary colors have been aligned in a grid and used in equal proportion, and therefore equal strength. The effect they produce is a changing pattern of cruciform shapes as each color achieves a temporary dominance.

1

2

2 Although the dominant color on this cover should be the overall green, the inclusion of a spot of red dominates the main color, deflecting the eye from the main image.

3 This design for a word puzzle makes obvious use of the tension that is achieved by applying complementary colors in close proximity to one another. The tonal equilibrium of the colors creates a visual contest for the eye. To solve the puzzle you follow the numbers to form the word "Rätsel", which means puzzle!

Photographic Style: Black and White

IN THE PAST, photography set itself apart from the mainstream of graphic design, and photographers were engaged as an accessory to the graphic process. But now it has become a prominent ingredient in graphic design, equal in importance to the other components. Indeed, certain periods have regarded photography as the predominant component, overshadowing typography, illustration and other design elements. Today, however, each component of a design tends to receive the same degree of attention.

AS A HISTORICAL STYLE

Black and white photography goes back to the birth of the medium and so is both a good historical record of past styles of design and documentary evidence of the changing styles in photography itself. Where the aim is to create a period or classic style, black and white images are perfectly appropriate. Sepia or hand-tinted prints, which were in vogue before the advent of color photography, can also be used to give a distinctive and classic look.

MODIFYING PHOTOGRAPHY

With black and white photography, it is also important to remember that once the image has been captured on film it can be modified in the darkroom to achieve a wide range of visual effects. Processing can be varied and the print can be made on different kinds of paper, including textured. Line and tone techniques can be used, and many other creative options are available.

Selecting the right photographer or the right photographic style for the job in hand is the key to producing a successful design.

1

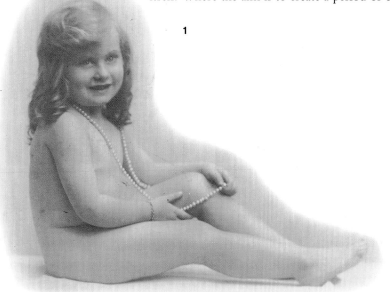

1 Soft-focus black and white photography, given a sepia patina, can suggest a bygone era. This photograph is, in fact, not a reproduction but an original.

2

3

4

2 Old photographs can be embellished with other graphic elements and reused in a modern context. The grainy appearance of the image and its extreme tonal contrast have been heightened to evoke a particular period.

3 Modern black and white photography is capable of simulating images from the past. This photograph of a girl has a hint of sepia which gives it a romantic, long-ago atmosphere.

4 A useful technique of black and white image-making is seen in this modern photograph that has been hand-tinted to give the impression of a faded 1950s shot.

Photographic Style: Color and Tints

WITH THE ARRIVAL of color photography, a new period in design began. With its power to reproduce reality, the medium revolutionized image making. Most modern color photographers can be identified by the style of their work, which can guide the designer in establishing the right approach to a project.

MANIPULATING PHOTOGRAPHY

The color in a photograph can be manipulated to create a specific effect. The lighting, for example, can be arranged so as to maximize or minimize its intensity. Different speeds of film will also affect the rendition of colors. Furthermore, modern processing techniques make it possible to stipulate how the component colors of a picture should be treated. For example, a particular color can be emphasized to a very specific degree. Often, the success of a photograph depends on the technical control exercised during processing.

The designer can arrange for a color photograph to be printed in a particular color or colors. There are some photographers who specialize in unconventional approaches to color, and their work can be used to give individuality to a project. The scope for using straight and manipulated color photographs is so broad that the designer should not find it difficult to keep within the brief.

ART DIRECTION

Ultimate control over the appearance of the photograph lies with the designer, who must define its shape, size and proportions before embarking on the design. It is during the art direction, which can be the sole responsibility of the designer, that the elements within the photograph are deployed according to the demands of the planned design. This leaves the photographer to exercise his or her creative skills to produce a photograph in the style desired.

1

1 Color photography can be art-directed to emphasize a design style, and to pinpoint a market. The color can be finely tuned during processing to enhance the visual effect.

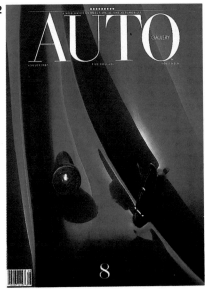

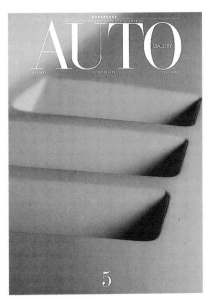

SHOULD'VE GONE TO SASSOON'S

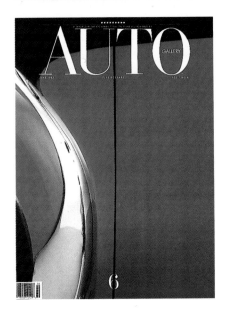

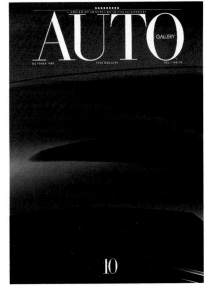

2 The enormous scope of creative photography enables designs to concentrate on a particular aspect of graphic design. Color and almost abstract shapes have been isolated in this work to create a sequence of coordinated covers.

3 A great deal of creative planning can go into a simple image such as this, which communicates its message so effectively. Here the idea is enhanced by the sophistication of the photographic style.

4 Color photography can be used to exaggerate natural qualities. With careful styling, skilled lighting and arrangement of subject matter to balance the color and composition, it is possible to achieve dramatic effects.

Photographic Style: Special Effects

FOR THE DESIGNER, the creation of a photograph does not stop with the release of the shutter. The new technology makes it possible to produce a limitless range of special post-camera effects. Many interesting avant-garde publications have established themselves by producing innovative and exciting designs with specially adapted photographs.

PHOTOCOPIES

Modern photocopying machines, with their ability to reproduce photographs with all the tonal qualities excluded, have formed the basis of some interesting and creative visual effects. As photocopying technology progresses toward full-color reproduction, with dot screens and textured meshes, so the possibilities for the designer expand. Painting and tinting, and cutting and tearing photocopies are such inexpensive techniques that anyone can experiment with them.

OTHER TECHNIQUES

Line-converted photography (that is, with all tones between black and white removed) is certainly not new, and many specialist and traditional production houses offer interesting and sometimes unique ways of converting photographic images into illustrations.

Montage is a popular method of combining a number of photographs in a single image. A direct, even brutal, approach can lead to stylish effects. With the use of modern computers, the technique of montage has reached new levels of refinement.

You will probably find the appropriate type of special photographic effect for your project within the various techniques now available, and the scope for innovation grows all the time. The development of this field is largely fueled by the demands of a young, sophisticated market.

1

1 This advertisement illustrates how a monochromatic photograph can be used to set a scene, while the product is cleverly isolated in color.

dobber®
1961
TIMELESS TRADITION

2

3 The photography in this design
has been softened by removing
the harsher colors, but retaining a
rose-pink hue that gives an air of
modern sophistication.

3

Today Magazine
volume Three
number One february
nineteen hundred
Eighty Seven
Dayton Hudson
Department Stores
All About Spring

2 What appears to be a black and
white image was in fact made by a
full-color printing process. The
image was produced on a black
and white transparency and then
scanned in full color and printed.

4 Montaging photographs can
take many forms as the print
process can be used to
manipulate and change a single
image into multiple images. These
can then be printed in colors
appropriate to the required style.

4

Background is a 4-color pixellation   computer-converted from B&W print

Illustration Style: Black and White

CHECKLIST
- Start a library of various styles of illustration.
- Subdivide this library into different techniques.
- Assess how they can be used for different markets.
- Study the historical development of line drawings.
- Investigate how these techniques can be applied to modern work.

ILLUSTRATION IS AS varied and versatile as the individuals who produce it, and most illustrators have an identifiable style. Black and white illustrations are commonly used in daily newspapers and periodicals. From the drawings found in black and white press advertisements to the stylishly avant-garde work used to support editorial features, there are a wide range of attractive and adaptable illustration styles. However, as their careers progress, illustrators tend to become identified with a specific field and most of their work will be for a particular market or medium.

ILLUSTRATORS

Most professional illustrations have a specific appeal and are best used only in an appropriate context. It is the task of the designer to find an illustrator whose style suits that of the project in hand. However, some illustrators are renowned for their willingness to accept a challenge and tackle a project that lies outside their normal repertoire.

1, 2 and 3 Even a skilled illustrator needs to be art-directed to make sure that the illustration is appropriate to the ethos of the design. As the examples clearly show, a single subject can be manipulated in a variety of ways to achieve the right style.

4 Many techniques are available to create a distinctive style, including linocut, woodcut, scraper board, silhouettes, pen and ink and line drawings. In these illustrations, with their woodcut effect, there is an intriguing ambiguity between the classic technique of the woodcut and the ultramodern style of illustration.

4

5 Illustration can be used in such a way that the overall design hinges on it. The use of black and white in these bags derives from the woodcut style illustrations.

5

6

6 A linocut or similar technique could be used to imitate the traditional woodcut style of this example.

Illustration Style: Single Color

COLOR CAN BE used in a design in its flat, opaque form or more expansive use can be made of it by changing its density with different grades of tint. More important, color can provide a visual link between the illustration and the other elements of the overall design. It can also be exploited to isolate a particular feature of the illustration, highlighting it and giving it individuality.

Color, either integrated into or added to an illustration, allows the designer to recreate specific period styles. For example, a simple line illustration can be transformed into an ageing drawing by the use of a subtle hint of sepia tone.

In some designs, color is used to create an overall background. This is a useful application, as it enables the designer to reverse out elements. Obviously, if the design is printed on white paper, then these elements will be white, but you could consider printing on colored paper or card, which can be very effective.

MAKING A CHOICE

Choosing a color that suits the style of your design requires great care, since it must reflect the nature and quality of the product or service it promotes, and appeal to a specific group of consumers. Assess the range of colors currently used to advertise similar products or services, and learn from them. But do not imitate them slavishly, since it is better to pursue a solution that combines effectiveness with originality.

1, 2, & 3 These three illustrations are of the same subject, but the different techniques combined with different colors give a different period feel.

4

Public Information Graphics

In collaboration with
The British Council
at the International
Language Centre
Rue de la Vallee 6
Dalstraat Brussels

9·30-12·30/4·00-7·00
Monday to Friday

28 March-27 April
(closed Easter week)

Design: Banks and Miles

DIEU ET MON

6

5

4 The prominence of elements can be changed by controlling their visual balance with color. The overall yellow background of this piece of work dominates the eye, whereas the illustration is made passive by producing it in a soft red.

5 This stylized illustration, in the vein of Matisse and Picasso, uses line to describe the subject, and color in slabs to indicate the environment.

6 Traditional European illustration is implied in this childrenswear logo. The color reinforces the image, conveying a sense of quality and permanence.

Illustration Style: Full Color

FULL-COLOR ILLUSTRATION embraces an immense range of styles, from realism to the bizarre and fantastic. It therefore gives the designer ample scope for presenting graphic images in fresh and unique ways. Since the days of watercolor, color illustration has evolved to include the use of many different mediums. Although these tend to produce their own styles, they can also be applied to the images of the past. Indeed, much modern illustration combines current techniques with bygone imagery in an attempt to breathe life into established products in a fickle and demanding age.

MAKING A CHOICE

The designer makes important decisions about the nature of the color illustration to be used when evaluating all the elements of the design. The intended prominence of the illustration, and how it is to be displayed, will affect the designer's choice of illustration style. A design can be aimed at different target audiences by exploiting color illustration. For example, the lid of a chocolate box may carry an overall dark and moody color. The inclusion of a carefully commissioned drawing can give the product an appeal to a different market.

1 The illustration produced for any design must be related to or reflected in the supporting design elements. The style and technique can be used to echo a particular period or image and in such cases the illustration should be conceived with this aim in mind.

2 When the design elements are brought together, further control can be exercised over their positioning and relative proportions.

3

3 and 4 The illustration of the coat of arms serves to remind us of the traditional quality of this beer.

4

5

5 The illustration and type reflect a nostalgic, pre-war style of German illustration.

6 This paradoxical and humorous juxtaposition of a Renaissance merchant and the

Mastercard suggests that among the man's possessions is a modern credit card. The style of illustration evokes with precision the painting styles of this period.

6

7

Fine English Country Soap made from a natural base and Cherry Kernel Oil. Introduced by the Romans the Cherry Tree has become a favourite for its blossom and rich fruit.

7 An eighteenth-century French illustration depicting a cherry orchard is accompanied by a black-ink drawing and hand-tinted colors. The central illustration is delicately painted in color with no black added, to contrast with the orchard scene. A hint of color in the background links the type and illustration, creating a charming traditional style.

THE MAKING OF STYLE

CENTRAL TO ACHIEVING the right design for the market is the way the visual components are chosen, assembled and displayed. The first part of this book showed landmarks in the evolution of design styles, each a classic example of its time. By studying the visual information of the past, you can learn how to produce subtle and effective designs for today's markets.

THINK ABOUT MARKETS

In the second part of the book, you read a brief introduction to some of the elements that together produce style. There are no rules that govern the combination of these elements, and the designer must rely on those insights gained when trying to determine the kind of design that is most likely to appeal to the intended target audience.

So much of the success of a design style in reaching its market depends on how well the designer is attuned to that audience, and how good he or she is at maintaining enthusiasm during the rigors of solving the design problem.

UNITY OF DESIGN

In this third part of the book, you can learn how the various elements of design interlock to produce an established style. Notice how each element, from typeface to illustration, complements or molds the other elements, lending a unity to the design.

`The work featured represents a wide variety of talents from the world of professional graphic design. The great variety in approach is clear, and you should also be able to discern the hand of individual designers. Each piece of work has been categorized according to its market image, the governing force that influenced the designer's decisions. However, even within these market categories, there is a good deal of variation. This is because the sort of person the product is aimed at determines the style, and this question – who is it aimed at? – is by no means a simple one. For instance, a label for a jar of pickles may have a traditional image, but who actually buys pickles? The amount of market research that *could* be done on this topic is infinite and as the answer changes as it becomes more detailed, the design will be modified. This question – who buys this? – must be asked in relation to each of the categories of style presented. In each case the design should be analyzed closely in order to understand the formulae applied.

Traditional Style

WHEN A CLIENT's brief demands a "traditional" appeal for a product or service, the designer must ask the client, and reflect on, exactly what this means, and then decide how it is to be interpreted. A traditional product or service may have an established track record with a clearly defined audience. Alternatively, if the product is new, the market into which it is going to fit will have been identified by research as a traditional outlet.

THE PRODUCT AND THE MARKET

A traditional product or service is usually a long-established one, which projects ideas of reliability, offers craftsmanship where appropriate, and displays professionalism in all cases. Furthermore, it gives a sense of permanence, reassuring its customers that their financial outlay has given them value and lasting quality. The customer also feels able to count on future purchases of the same product or service being of consistently high quality.

The consumers of a traditional product or service have no specific or set characteristics. The product or service generally appeals to a wide audience even if the product range is not suitable for all individuals. A hard sales approach rarely accompanies the promotion of traditional styles. It is not in any case necessary, for at some point in their lives, the traditional approach becomes attractive to most people. This is not to say that such products or services have a mass appeal. It is a case of the mood and awareness of the target audience moving toward the product rather than the reverse.

Logos are the embodiment of a company's style. The quality of the product or service offered by a company is often reflected in its corporate image. The designer must select this image carefully so that it accurately conveys that quality.

1 This design for a bakery contains all of the visual messages needed to establish a sense of secure, traditional values. Each of the elements incorporated in the design plays a vital role in telling the purchaser about the natural qualities of the product.

2 By isolating the colors chosen for this design, you can appreciate how the designer has carefully used them to complement the image of the product.

3 The typeface chosen for the main heading reflects all the qualities of a long-established product and reputation.

3

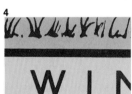

4 The supporting typeface is simple and effective, and letter spacing is used to recall the traditional styles of printing bread labels.

5

5 The simplicity of form of the central illustration suggests the natural goodness of a traditionally made quality product.

1

1 To appreciate the full effect of the Windmill Bakery design, you must consider the product as a whole. The lower part of the design carries the loaf in a basket-like container. The wrapper allows the purchaser to see the bread, making it an integral part of the design.

PUTTING IT TOGETHER

Having examined the characteristics of the product or service, how do you arrive at the right style for your design? What elements are likely to produce the right image in a fresh and modern way, while continuing to assure quality and reliability? There is no single answer to these questions – each design project has its own. In seeking the identity of the product, it is important to gain a knowledge of its qualities. Examine the images and associations that come to the surface in your visual research.

HELP FROM THE CLIENT?

Certain typefaces seem to have a natural affinity with the product, although you should always look for the less obvious approach, seeking to establish a similar relationship in an inventive, perhaps unique, way. This process relies on intuition as well as knowledge. Remember, too, that your client, with many years of nurturing the product or service, could be instrumental in uncovering some of the design solutions. The client may, however, be unable to identify the ethos of the particular market, and have a view conditioned exclusively by other business colleagues. It is therefore your job to research all the possible market factors and produce a design with a broad-based visual appeal.

2 This Harrods product again features the natural qualities of traditional baking. The combination of colors is clever, although it is certainly not an immediately obvious choice. However, the tones of purple add sophistication and blend with the

colors of the illustration. The typefaces give an idea of traditional craftsmanship and are depicted in a color which relates to the product. Subtle visual links relate one part of the design to another, for example, the portrait emphatically reinforces the traditional rustic image.

1 This food pack has been created with a limited use of color and communicates its visual message with directness and crisp efficiency while retaining an overall feeling of tradition and quality.

The typography, using a traditionally based Bodoni style, links harmoniously with the drawing style of the illustration. The powerful style of the black and white illustration set on a gold background evokes an appropriate sense of richness and quality.

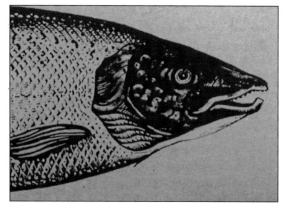

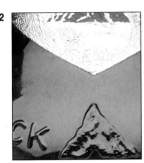

2 The packaging of this drink is typical of established beer containers, but cider, itself a "traditional" product, is not normally sold in this way. From the raised lettering on the glass to the outline hand-lettered style, there is the suggestion of a long-

established product. The illustration serves to reinforce the product's strong image and quality, and is echoed throughout the design. The company logo is applied as if it were a traditional seal of quality.

1 An original packaging concept for a traditional leisure product: jigsaw puzzles. The container acts both as a practical means of storage and an attractive display. The contents of the puzzle pack were designed to coordinate with the image of the label. The puzzles are exquisitely drawn, with all the quality and detail of traditional draftsmanship from which the product springs.

2 Hand-made foods need an image that defines their individual flavor and quality. These products are faithful to their origins by virtue of the carefully chosen colored lid wrapping, which harmonizes with the overall background color of the label. The typography and illustration also conjure up the Victorian tradition of homemade country produce.

3 The hallmarks of quality and tradition are united in the use of gold borders and rustic reds. Type and illustration give a sense of the background and natural qualities of the drink, while delicately painted images are displayed together to convey an air of luxury.

4 This product, with its regal coat of arms, announces its traditional standing. Its quality is reflected in a multitude of complex images. Intricate borders imitate materials. Scrolls appear as three-dimensional features with illustration that depicts the high degree of individual attention given to producing the cigars. Each typeface expresses the same message in its own way.

Retrospective Style

IN RECENT YEARS, fashions in retrospective design style have changed in response to changing fashions in society. In the 1960s, the Art Nouveau images of the late 1800s featured prominently in all kinds of design. Since then, a broader sweep of periods is now evoked in the fashioning of retrospective style.

Retrospective styles have become fashionable in the promotion of products and services. To reflect specific qualities of a bygone age, designers strive to link images from the past with present-day styling in a way that can be widely understood. The products or services that are treated in this way may well have counterparts from the past that are familiar to the general public. For example, a present-day personalized dry-cleaning service can be related to the practice among wealthy Victorian men of having a valet.

SUITABILITY OF PRODUCT

The product or service itself, to be suitable for this approach, must possess certain qualities. It must appear convincing when depicted graphically, and must perform effectively in reality. But by no means does the styling need to be historically accurate. What it does need to achieve is a common ground that the public can relate to subliminally. Not all members of the public at whom the promotion is aimed will be in any way knowledgeable about the images used. However, this is not to say that they can be fooled, since they will have in common subconscious associations that the designer cannot afford to ignore. For example, since most modern families have photographs of their own recent past and perhaps of earlier generations, it is easy to play on this familiarity with the past by depicting bygone fashions and coloring the image to appear like an old photograph.

1 A number of corporate logos echo the styling of specific periods and design movements of this century: the industrialized lines of Art Deco, the machine-made image, the sporting fashions that recall an elegant past.

1

THE CORRECTED TEXT

ULYSSES

JAMES JOYCE

$11.95 /394-74312-1

2 James Joyce's controversial masterpiece has been designed over the years in many forms. This modern version echoes the historic changes seen in Soviet art early this century. The style, reminiscent of the work of El Lissitzky, is suitably applied to the revolutionary work of this great author. The typefaces are boldly functional, with colors that give solidity to the design. The only departure from the formal design is the angled panel that deliberately breaks with the geometric pattern.

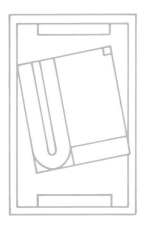

1 These matchbox labels draw their strength from two distinctive pictorial devices: the historic machines of the early years of travel, and the stylized drawing imitating the work of Cassandre.

THE ELEMENTS

Certain letterforms can recall the past, suggesting, for example, the saloons of the Wild West or the early American circus. The method of printing itself can be selected to evoke the desired associations. Fuzzy or broken characters conjure up the time when smooth, uniform typesetting was not yet available.

To identify the appropriate elements to be used in the styling of your project, it is important to research the selected period thoroughly for effective visual components. Once you are fully immersed in the period, you will have some mobility in your choice of elements. You will also find that you can bend the rules by using modern counterparts. What you will be doing is not accurately recreating the period, but giving it a facelift so that it suits today's audience.

2 This menu design uses the imagery of the past in a considered manner, thus retaining the individual quality of each image. The illustrations are lovingly displayed like cut-outs that might be found on an old Victorian screen. No embellishment seems to have been added, and each of the items seems to be an original in its own right. The added information cleverly blends with the illustrations. The reproduction of color retains the softness of early printed work.

3 The contents of the menu are displayed as an overlay separated from the collage background. However, the elements are united by the cut-out lady who overlaps with the information.

1 This box label could be mistaken for the Californian orange boxes of the early twentieth century. The design and illustration technique reflect the images and painting styles of these early designs. However the modern design is free to use a surreal approach, changing the realistic oranges into popsicles. The typography, with its outline white-out letters, imitates its historical source.

1

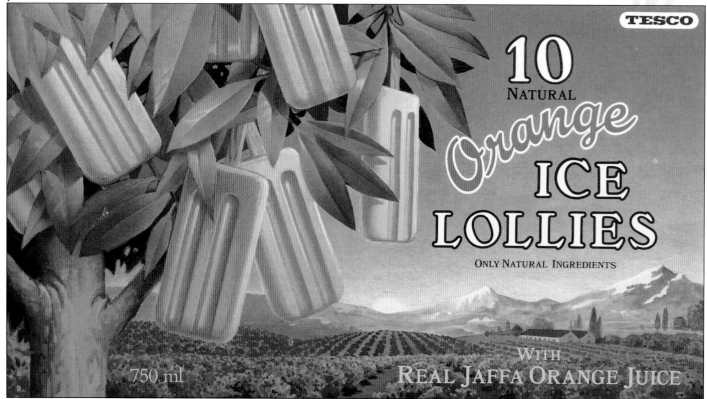

2

2 A range of display and packaging materials promoting the delicate scent bottle. The style of illustration (which appears to tell a story) echoes the work of the Pre-Raphaelites, and the gentle colors suggest a patina of age and quality.

3

3 The Gauloise cigarette pack has its own classic design style. This modern pack design continues the tradition of blue and white. By retaining the familiar typefaces and linking them with the image of the car, the designer has evoked a sense of elegance and timelessness.

1 The distinctive type is reminiscent of the styles of the late 1920s and early 1930s, with curves that are flattened to create elongated linear forms. The geometric shapes created by borders and type are carefully engineered to make squared-up shapes and patterns.

2 A design that recalls the images used in early issues of *Vogue,* which in turn drew inspiration from artists such as Toulouse-Lautrec. The typography is kept stylish and simple to complement the illustration.

4 This modern interpretation of Art Deco styling, with simplified illustrative buildings, formal reversed borders and opposing typefaces, creates a distinctive European image harking back to the early 1930s.

2

4

1

3 This design for a new range of products captures the ethos of modern leisure pursuits while depicting them in the context of the past.

3

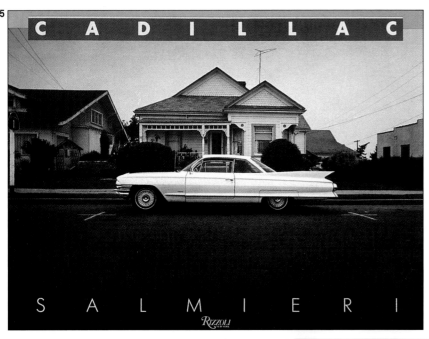

5 The design for this piece hinges around the central theme of the 1950s Cadillac. The photography appears to be from that period, as the colors have faded and have a rather unreal quality.

CHECKLIST
- Identify the period that best suits the brief.
- Research images from the chosen period.
- What characteristics of the period are common to your overall theme?
- Visualize how your audience will respond to the images.
- What are the underlying implications of the images you intend to use?
- Build up your design from the carefully selected elements.
- Produce alternative designs using these elements, varying the emphasis.
- Which of these retrospective designs has the widest appeal?

6 Packaging design borrowed directly from Victorian England. The typefaces are faithful to the style of that time, and the association is enhanced by the delicate hint of tinted pastel color.

7 A modern product packaged to evoke the beers of another era. The images of the distinctive hand pump and the steam train, and the complementary typeface, work together to this end.

Classic Style

A DESIGN THAT has a classic appeal is inevitably an historically important piece of work, a masterpiece of its time. Throughout history there have been designers who have created memorable and exemplary pieces of work with both stature and longevity. Such designs, from whatever sector of the design industry they come, have attracted much attention. In some cases their flouting of convention distanced them at first from what was generally acceptable. What is striking about these designs is their unique and often unforgettable visual qualities.

CLASSIC GRAPHIC DESIGN

Classic designs can emerge from any sector of the market. The VW "Beetle" started life as a functional, inexpensive car produced for a mass market. The Rolls Royce, with its distinctive grill and "flying lady" mascot, has long been a symbol of luxury. Both car designs have achieved classic status. In graphic design certain pieces of work have the same quality of permanence as the "Beetle" and the Rolls Royce. Internationally recognized products such as Coca Cola, Pepsi Cola, and Perrier have survived through the sheer quality of their design. Logos of long-established companies, although they may be restyled to suit modern tastes, usually retain a strong suggestion of the quality that made them so original in the past, and has guaranteed their continuing success. Strictly speaking, a classic design should be distinguished from one that is better described as classical. At one time, the latter referred exclusively to a piece of work that conjures up the spirit of ancient Greece or Rome in its simple, harmonious, well-proportioned and restrained style. However, in recent times the terms have been used interchangeably.

Images that have become classics in their own time are captured in some very distinctive company logos. As the years pass, their visual appeal remains unchanged. Timeless designs such as these often faithfully reflect the qualities inherent in the service or product they promote.

1 The classical associations evoked by this design have been achieved by the choice of subjects and by the photographic treatment, which has echoes of an ancient sophistication and wisdom. A delicate and sensitive design, yet with a profound emotional impact.

2 The simple timeless elegance of this design reveals the confident and thoughtful approach to structure and geometrical balance that is necessary to communicate classic qualities.

eighteenth century. Colors blend within the design to give stately elegance to the historical theme. The geometric structure underpinning the design is an essential part of its strength.

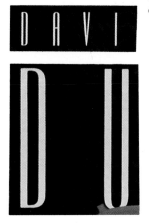

1 To appreciate the harmony within a design you need to isolate each of the elements in order to analyze the quality it portrays. In this design, an historical illustration is finely balanced with modern typography chosen to evoke the classical styling of the

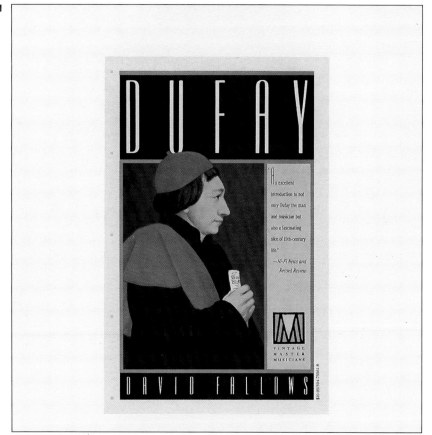

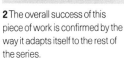

2 The overall success of this piece of work is confirmed by the way it adapts itself to the rest of the series.

THE CLASSICAL HERITAGE

Many designs rely heavily on the classical (Greek/ Roman) heritage, most notably by displaying a noble elegance with minimal adornment. Once you have grasped the nature of the visually classical, the elements required for a design expressing this mood almost select themselves. Typefaces should be sensitive and slender, confident but not extrovert. Your borders can be quietly lyrical, and your colors

3 This uniquely effective idea, created with bold simplicity, defies time. Each of the illustrations has been constructed with care and precision, and although they differ, they relate perfectly to one another within the design.

should be similarly restrained. Illustration can be molded to suit classical themes, but photography, being a relatively modern design element, must be used with discretion and in a subdued way. Avoid at all costs the mere parody of classical style that results from insensitive design.

UNDERSTANDING CLASSICS

Returning to the classic design, the same caution applies. To reinterpret a classic style you must respect and retain the major features of the original design; otherwise, you will produce a diluted, even burlesque, version of it. You need to understand the structures that underlie the classic design. Abram Games said that good design can be likened to good engineering: the invisible understructure should be as well designed as what you can see. Always consider the underlying structure before you apply decoration, and then make sure that the latter is appropriate.

Luncheon

Cold Appetizers

Terrine of Duc

Sev

A Selection of Smo

1 This package of information, designed to appeal to a sophisticated audience, sets a tone of high social standing.

The classic marbled effect used throughout for borders and surface designs gives the design a formal, coordinated elegance. The central illustration depicting the "Sport of Kings" confirms the

target audience. Typography is formally arranged with luxurious space surrounding the information.

1

2 This wine list, designed to appeal to first class air travelers, benefits from a fine balance of elegant typography and distinctive modern illustration. The text is set in a harmonious combination of copperplate type and traditional serif faces that conveys a sense of high quality and luxury.

1 A feast of color created to depict the established quality of products sold by Fortnum and Mason of London by echoing painting styles of centuries past.

2 The quality of this internationally-recognized classic design does not deteriorate with time.

3 A minimum of design elements used effectively and reflected in the construction of the package. As the box is opened, it echoes the motif of the crescent.

4 Sophistication and elegance achieved with simple but carefully proportioned reversed-out type on a smoky gray surface. Two italic letters give the formal design a lyrical feel.

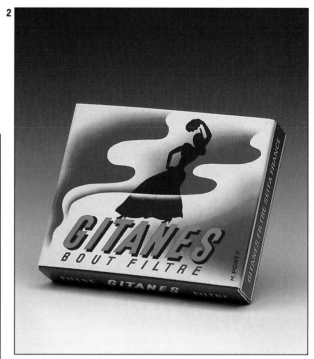

5

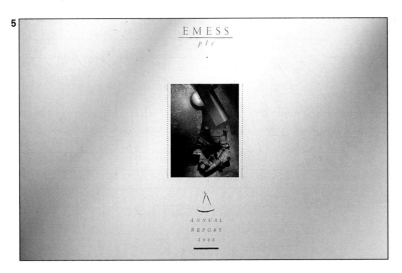

5 The luxury of white space has been used to emphasize the elegance of classic typography while the photographic image illustrates old equipment used in marine navigation. (The objects were chosen for their mellow brown colors which create an atmosphere of age.) The photograph acts as a window cutout strategically placed within the design space.

6 The use of modern illustration to package classical music breaks away from convention. At the same time, these designs exploit classic qualities in type, creating a unique blend of original imagery.

CHECKLIST

■ Decide what images are likely to relate to your product or service.

■ Seek out all kinds of image from the relevant period.

■ Identify some graphic styles of the period.

■ The majority of images available are those that have survived because of their classic qualities. Study these qualities.

■ Apply the styling carefully to your own work.

■ What similar design elements are still available today?

■ Remember, your interpretation should echo the past but be relevant to the styles of today.

6

Young Style

PERHAPS THE BROADEST and most innovative area of design is that aimed at the young, a market that ranges from the toddler to the sophisticated young adult.

DESIGNING FOR CHILDREN

Taking the youngest age group first, you must be able to relate to the current trends that influence children. Unfortunately, there is no definitive image, rather a welter of images provided by television, films, books and comics, pop music and the children's contemporaries. Clearly, the graphic styles that appeal most to children are those that are colorful and inventive. However, the images you select must also relate to the children's knowledge and experience, and this is why it is necessary to understand the influences on their lives.

The older the age group you are designing for, the greater the challenge. Images become harder to discover, and the work requires even greater subtlety. Older children normally have a very good eye for detail and are capable of spotting a poor imitation at a glance. This means that promotions using their current heroes are best when closely based on original source material. Most children no longer rely totally on their parent's advice and are often independent in their choices. While recognizing this fact, you should also attempt to appeal to the parents' sense of responsibility.

1 Companies that promote products aimed at the young must consider carefully the image they themselves project, not least in their corporate identity. Modern typefaces and associated visual elements are used to capture the mood of the moment. Little importance is placed on the lasting quality of the image, although some images become the vogue for many generations.

1

2 If they are to communicate to a young audience, the elements of the design and the colors used

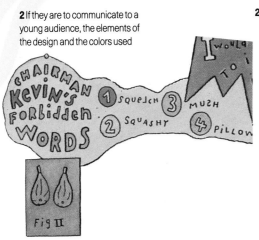

must be appropriate to the target age group and its level of comprehension. Here, the stylized illustration of both lettering and graphic shapes are combined in a busy and interesting format. The

cut-out head, recalling punk art, breaks down the photographic style into dots and colored tints, and can be clearly identified with its target market.

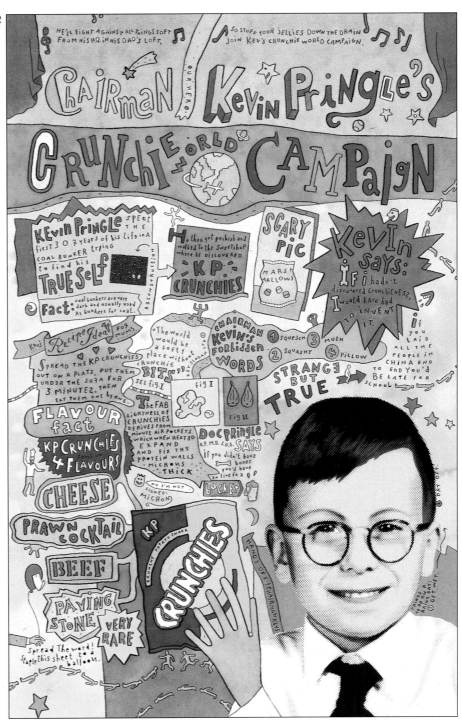

1 This sales leaflet produced for a British bank appeals to a young market through a blend of carefully arranged images. Nostalgic, retrospective color worn by high-fashion, casual youngsters is punctuated with typography reflective of modern youth cult magazines.

DESIGNING FOR TEENAGERS

The teenage market presents different problems in styling, as tastes at this age range from the ostentatious to the highly sophisticated. However, most teenagers aspire to the values of an age group that is just above theirs. This fact should guide your research and should be reflected in the design you create.

Pop culture, as seen on television and video, provides most of the styles that younger teenagers relate to. But by their mid-teens, they are looking for new, perhaps mysterious, images. At this age the young person has a self-conscious desire to be seen as an individual, while still being identifiable as belonging to a group.

Images that appeal to the mid-teen group range right across the visual field, from the arty to the mundane. In recent years fantasy images and drawings such as those by Roger Dean and Boris Vallejo have enjoyed great popularity among this group. A more sophisticated but equally popular approach can be seen in, for example, the television advertisements for Levi 501 jeans.

The older teenage market demands highly creative, often unusual, styles of design. Classical heroes, trendy technology, or anarchic visions – any source of themes can be plundered to meet the demands of this market, with its vast spending power, for impressive, convincing and, above all, original styles.

2 Hand-tinting black and white photography can give the impression that the photograph is very old. This device aims to relate to a style-conscious audience. A traditional product intended to embrace both the young and the fashion-conscious adult market by using smart, fashionable graphics that hint at quality and lasting reputation.

1 Magazines for the young adult represent an important attempt at achieving the right style of image to communicate with this age group. This magazine, with its arty appearance, sets a style for the young, aware, fashion-conscious reader. An adventurous use of image and color can be found in editorial matter, photography and advertisements. Typographically, it sets itself apart from mainstream images through exciting experimentation.

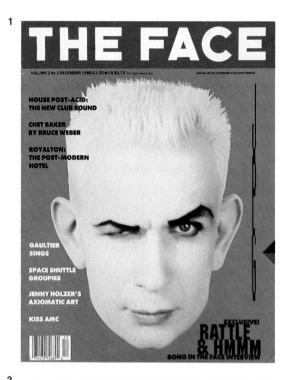

2 Magazines aimed at young people offer a striking array of visual choices. The layouts and colors applied to *Blitz* contrast with those of *The Face*. *Blitz* uses white space and more traditional layout in its appeal to a different sector of the youth market.

YOUNG ADULT MARKET

Styling for the young adult market requires a further degree of sophistication, but must also take account of the wide variation in taste and spending power that becomes apparent at this age. Your design could be for anything from a Porsche to pre-packed snack foods, but each product requires a highly tuned and aggressive technique to project it in an extremely competitive market place.

When researching the influences on the young adult group, investigate the images they respond to by seeking out the obscure as well as the popular publications they read. Often the designers for the younger market are themselves the new generation of designers. It is therefore worth looking at their work for the shape of the styling of the future. Another approach is to style the work in a way that shocks the senses. Successful work of this kind both creates a new, unique identity and attracts the young consumer by departing from what is seen as boring and conventional.

The elements used in styling for the young consumer range from bubblegum lettering to high-technology type and digitalized illustration. New photographic and illustration styles appear all the time. The designer must keep in touch with what is new if he or she is to produce designs that appeal exclusively to this powerful sector of the market.

Cropped jacket, bra top,
wide trousers, shoes and belt
all by Ritzi Ozbek at Browns,
23-27 South Molton St
London W1

Bat-sleeved mini-dress by
Emilio Cavallini at Stone, 7a
Market St, Nottingham and
The Warehouse, 61-65
Glassford St, Glasgow

3

3 Each of the page layouts in *The Face* is treated as a further opportunity to convey a specific image. The layout and style of these fashion photographs relies on black and white to generate a casual ambience, while the addition of color conveys a sense of exclusivity to a trendy audience.

4

4 In this catalogue Italian fashions for the young are promoted in a documentary style by means of black and white photography. The nostalgic quality of the fashions and pictures is strongly emphasized by the use of tinted and vignetted images.

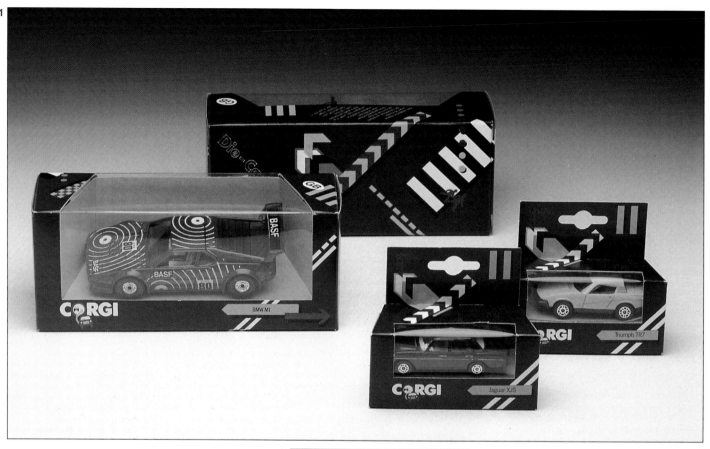

1 This modern packaging for toy cars uses bold imagery based on road signs and symbols. The design has a double function: the window shows the product off to its young audience, while the sophisticated packaging has a wider appeal to the older purchaser.

2 This long-established magazine was recently restyled to attract a younger readership. As a trade magazine its function is to appeal to younger recruits to the fashion trade, thereby securing its own future.

3 The typeface and the layout of copy in this promotion for a fashion company have a subversive quality, with photographic imagery that is provocative and has a hint of trendiness.

4 This high-fashion, avant-garde magazine creatively explores unusual photography techniques, integrating them with typographic layouts. Color is somber and restrained and sets out to create an intellectual aura. The overall image, intended to appeal to a highly refined audience, evokes a dedication to lofty ideals.

5 This brand-new magazine takes youth styling and applies it in a visually coherent and eloquent way. The montage of slim illustrations clearly defines the content and there is a cover background image that combines tradition with new design thought. The masthead typography is intended to communicate to an up-to-date, young and stylish market.

Mass-Market Style

BEFORE PREPARING A design for the mass market, you must first consider at which sector of this market your product or service is aimed. You must also be aware of its "unique selling point" (USP).

LOOKING AT THE PRODUCT

Nearly every product or service has an identity that distinguishes it from its competitors. To appeal to the mass market, the styling of your design has to bridge the divisions between different sectors of the public. In short, its appeal must be universal. A good design will express honestly and clearly the qualities inherent in what is on offer. In the case of supermarket products, given the wide choices available, the best kind of design is that which communicates the product's function in a straightforward and factual way. In this area of design, color and illustration are commonly used simply as a means of making the product stand out.

BRAND NAMES

Today's designer must also take advantage of product branding. In a product distinguished in this way, quality and consistency are guaranteed by the corporate name. Often, a new addition to a family of products or services is more likely to succeed when linked to a familiar brand name than when launched under an unknown brand name as a completely new product.

Brand-name companies can become very protective about the identity of their products. A good example of this occurred when a leading design company was asked to redesign the label on Heinz's famous baked-bean can. The company cleverly produced 57 effective designs, all of which were appropriate and differed visually from the original. But so cautious was Heinz that it decided in the end to change only the type style. Once you have captured your mass market, it is wisest to continue to give it familiar, identifiable images.

At the other end of the product scale, the opposite can apply. In the case of cars, the brand name is pre-eminent in reassuring the purchaser of the qualities he or she is buying. But while the public may not want to see their baked beans look different, they do want to see changes in the design of cars, and so the graphics used to promote new models must also change. The single element from the old promotional material most likely to feature prominently in the new design will be the company logo.

1 Mass-market branding is normally identified by a powerful logo or motif. Corporate identities project a mass-market image that gives an assurance of price, quality and dependability to different social groups.

1

2 The elements of a design with mass appeal may be repackaged many times to keep up with changes in public demand. To give a product fresh life the design for the contents can be reshaped with a distinctive (perhaps new) message, either to retarget an existing audience or to capture a larger audience. This package

design reflects its European roots. The typography has an implied French style and the illustration suggests simply and directly the delights of the French café. Both packs have been colour-coded to emphasize their differences.

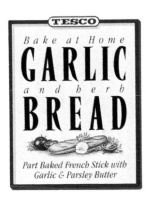

2

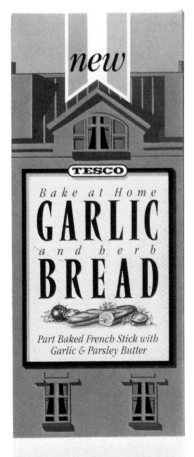

1 This container was designed so that the message on the label could be read both upright and sideways, as the designer was aware that he had no control over how it would be displayed in the shop.

FAMILIARITY

Generally, the public is reassured by familiar, favored images, and this important fact should be borne in mind when you choose' your design elements. Clearly, typefaces need to be appropriate in style to the product, but, more importantly, must communicate effectively and reassuringly. Colors must be chosen that reflect and emphasize the best qualities of the product or service. Remember, though, that fashions in colors can be irrelevant to an established or traditional product that requires years of sales to be generated by the styling you produce.

ILLUSTRATION AND PHOTOGRAPHY

In much mass-market advertising, illustration plays a supportive role in the design by reinforcing the projected image or catching the eye of new customers. However, photography is a greater force in the promotion of products and services, and a vast choice of styles, effects and image classification can be achieved. It is important in all cases to select the right photographer for the work, and to provide a clear and precise brief.

2 Competing with brand leaders is among the greatest of design challenges. The task is to create a design that reflects the best qualities of a product while giving the potential customer the confidence to change to a new brand. This product states clearly and plainly its function as well as challenging its competitors with colorful and reassuring illustration.

AUTOMATIC ·

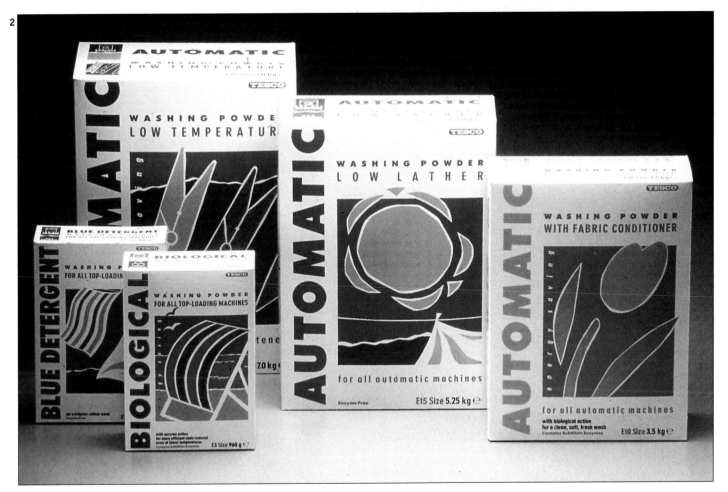

1 When leading brand names compete in the market, the designer needs to make sure not only that the graphics attract the right attention, but also that the design and practicalities of the container have been fully worked out.

MARKETING PLOYS

In the promotion of mass-market products, it is common to see current personalities, events or seasonal factors brought into play. This ploy is normally used to complement the overall design and has the aim of focusing public attention more keenly on the product. However, the styling of the product itself remains constant. Contests have also become common as a means of promoting interest in the product by offering incentives while focusing at a subliminal level on the product's qualities.

Mass-market styling is so vast and varied a field that each sector, from promoting a light bulb to designing a popular magazine, requires specialized but stimulating research. Finding a style that has universal appeal calls for insight and judgment, and the challenge is best met by detailed study of the images that have achieved success in today's mass markets.

2 Seasonal products face the problem of being quickly forgotten. This new design for a long-established manufacturer guarantees lasting attention with its dazzling use of full-color graphic images. The central typography, which is applied as a logo device, gives continuity and identity to each of the products in the range. This type, hand created, relates directly to the function of the product itself. The background illustration used almost like wrapping paper is again depicted in individual colors to give variety and sparkle to the entire brand range.

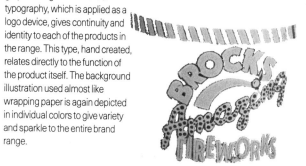

2

1 Sophistication can be applied in a controlled manner to mass-market products. The illustration, reflecting current fashions in mass art, serves as a visual message to accompany the photograph of the product.

2 The composition used to set a theme for a group of products can provide unity and consistency. In this line of snack food, the same composition and layout are reflected in each of the products.

3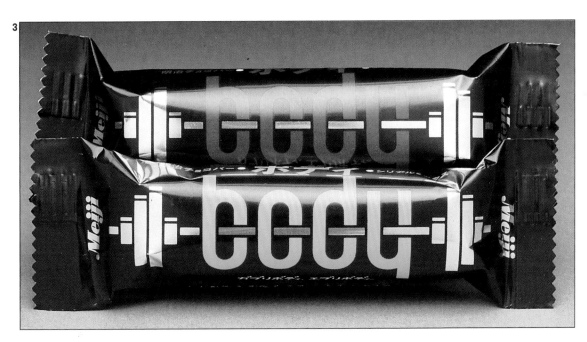

3 The name of a new product needs to say something that marks it out from its competitors. This product gives the impression that it will encourage fitness and health through nourishment.

5 This famous product has undergone many facelifts through the decades, only to return to its historic and familiar badge. Guinness relies on tradition to retain a mass-market appeal.

4 It is no accident that the promotion of new brands or own-brands often exploits certain features of the products of close rivals, giving the potential purchaser the impression of buying an already familiar product.

4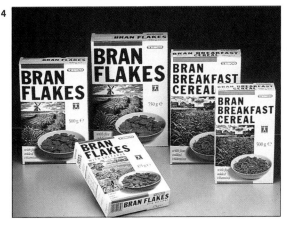

CHECKLIST

- Decide on the USP of the product or service.

- Take advantage of this feature in your design.

- Aim at as wide an appeal as possible.

- Present the product in an image that is as honest and factual as possible.

- Your product should have a unique appeal yet associate itself with the best of its competitors.

- The public is looking for consistency of quality, which should be reflected in the design.

- Choose the colors and typefaces that reflect the qualities of the product.

- All other graphic elements must support the active promotion of the product's inherent properties.

THE RIGHT STYLE FOR THE MARKET

BEFORE ANY DESIGN WORK begins, the designer must obtain from the client as full and as clear a picture as possible of the project to be undertaken. It is essential for both client and designer that this information is gathered thoroughly, regardless of how long it may take. Apart from helping the designer to achieve the desired effect, a clear brief is also important because a design that is in progress accumulates a range of expensive charges that will have to be met, whether the work is successful or not.

THE DESIGN BRIEF

It is ultimately your responsibility, as the designer, to establish the appropriate visual style for the client's market. At the briefing stage, however, you should avoid thrusting possible visual solutions on him in an attempt to show off the fertility of your own imagination. At the first briefing session treat the brief with the same detachment that you would employ when planning a long journey, for which every item of luggage has to be assessed in terms of usefulness and practicality.

Guidelines may already exist as to how a product should be presented. For example, a specific market place will have been established for most products,

and it is therefore a question of modeling the product so that it exploits this potential as fully as possible. Generally, it will be the client's wish for the product to become the market leader within its sphere. Some clients will have engaged the services of a market research organization to investigate public opinion and to determine people's preferences concerning the product or service. The designer should assess this market research thoroughly, making notes on its important features.

After the initial meeting you may feel that there is too much information to focus on. Look through it carefully, this time giving priority to the major aspects. Simplifying the information in this way produces the most effective results; the more complex you feel the project is, the more complex it will become. Keep it simple and it will communicate.

Look for the unique selling point (USP). If the product or service does not have one, create it. Maybe the product has something in its history that your client has overlooked, simply because he sees it as mundane or it does not accord with his own personal interests. Do not let this stop you from considering every aspect of the product with an objective eye. Your client will probably be less experienced in working closely with his product than his employees are, so he may lack what could be vital information in your search for the right style. Talk to long-serving employees and gain useful back-ground information from them. Tackle this stage of the project like a detective would treat an investigation, giving consideration to whatever pictures are conjured up in your mind. What seems at first irrelevant can sometimes be made into a wonderfully appealing feature.

Having exhausted all possible sources in your quest for information, you will now be in a position to assess what you have acquired. Focus on the strongest selling points and try to expand on them, making detailed notes as you do so. You may find that certain selling points appear to conflict, making it difficult to develop a style. On the other hand, a well-considered combination of two such points may provide an original solution. Discuss the full range of possibilities with your client before making any further decisions about the design.

Creating the Right Style

THE FINAL SECTION of this book presents a selection of individual approaches to problem solving in graphic design. It has been divided into four areas; design for the mass market; for the youth market; for sophisticated markets; and for markets that defy categorization.

STYLE AND MARKET

Each area is made up of case studies chosen for their variety of ideas and their appropriateness to their particular market. They allow you to see how internationally acclaimed designers tackle the problems of creating the right design style for new, well-established and popular products. You will learn how the designer deals with the complexities that each case study represents, and how attention is focused both on the projected audience and on the client's notion of how the product or service should be interpreted.

Each piece of work displays a unique approach by the designer. While one designer may seek inspiration from the qualities of type, space and shape, another will be influenced by external forces such as contemporary architecture or lifestyles. This is not to say that either of these approaches is evident in the final design, or that the designer has a blinkered view, for all graphic design relies on an environmental awareness as well as on the imagination. The broader the experience of the designer, the more he or she has to offer at the concept stage. Graphic design at its best complements the visual environment while fulfilling a specific function.

The purpose of these case studies is to cover as broad a spectrum as possible of the graphic design industry. Each piece of work solves a communication problem for a particular product or service. A great responsibility lies with the designer, for it is his or her task to create the right design for the right market. If the design fails, the designer has failed, too.

By learning how to design for a particular market, you will be on the way to creating a brand leader.

Mass Market: Case Studies

The first case study investigates the redesign of Harp lager in a market where its traditional brand image was becoming overshadowed by both new, more glamorous competitors and cheaper brands. Research by consumer testing proved that the product itself was not at fault and was competitive in taste and quality with other premium brands. A traditional brand loyalty was mainly exercised by a public whose purchase was driven more by habit than positive preference. The design objectives were to communicate an individual, contemporary, lively and exciting feel to the brand; to achieve maximum stand-out and impact in a crowded market, while retaining elegance and dignity; and to guarantee the product's immediate recognition as Harp.

Marie Claire is an upscale women's magazine with stylish page layouts and a mass appeal in Europe. The problem a designer faces with a magazine of this kind is continuity of image, given a large number of elements that all require meticulous presentation. The proportions of each element, and the space allocated to it, are conditioned by the overall image of the magazine and the designer's ability to manipulate this image with inventive and creative skill.

The third case study investigates the development of an entirely new product specifically devised to achieve brand leadership among a teenage audience. This product relies heavily on its name, which was the first major decision. Once this had been established, the creation of a design that prompted all the right emotional responses had to follow. The impact of this design was of paramount importance to its success, because it was felt that the target audience would be so involved in the style of the product that its content would take second place. It was also important that the image should be visually unique, so that promotional material would be instantly memorable.

1 In the initial stages it was decided to produce several possible designs. Clearly, some factors in the old image needed changing immediately. These first designs range from the evolutionary to some more revolutionary ideas. So that they could be evaluated and tested, these designs were mocked up in three different ways. First, they were produced in black and white, allowing the viewer to explore the shapes and layout created by the images. The second approach was to adopt the traditional Harp colors of blue and yellow. The third design applied the colors and elements in new and original proportions.

2 The same presentation formula was used on a number of design options. It became clear that a number of options were hindering the progress of this design. If the Harp identity was to be retained, it seemed necessary to keep the shape of the bottle label. A review of the market place revealed, however, that the new brand competitors were breaking this mold and setting new standards in the fashion of can design. They no longer tended toward "roundel" devices, and more reliance was placed on unique layout and overall color and image. In addition, the Harp colors of blue and yellow were felt to downgrade the product.

3 The experience of the previous designs led to a rethink of the overall concept, and the design moved away from the "bottle-badge" format. The colors were now applied in a much more striking and original way, but avoiding a clash that would cheapen the image. Warranties and signatures were included as these additions reinforced the product's new, authoritative tone.

4 It was now apparent that the best designs were predominantly blue and white, and so the yellow became a less obvious ingredient. Two of the designs here were selected for further development in which particular attention could be paid to the royal warranty and the choice of blue could be developed. The chevron ("V") device was particularly effective as it echoed the foil wrapping of premier bottled lagers.

5 There followed further development of the foil chevron, with a completely new concept for the type. The yellow was replaced with a rich golden bronze, and to add texture and a further dimension, a pattern imitating a regularly indented surface was introduced. The type shed all references to the Harp traditions and logo.

6 The final design, clearly emerging from previous concepts, embodied Harp's new move toward style, individuality and modernity. The new design made subtle use of the chevron, lending quality to the overall image. The Harp typography was retained largely in its original form and the graphic embellishments of seal and signature were applied with precision and finesse. The chevron creates an eye-catching pattern when displayed in quantity on the shelf.

marie

1 The first task of the designer is to establish the elements that will be used to create the design. *Marie Claire,* like most magazines, uses pre-printed layout grids on which the designer works up layout ideas. At this stage roughly drawn sketches can spark off ideas, helping the designer to visualize how elements can be arranged in different proportions, to create different shapes.

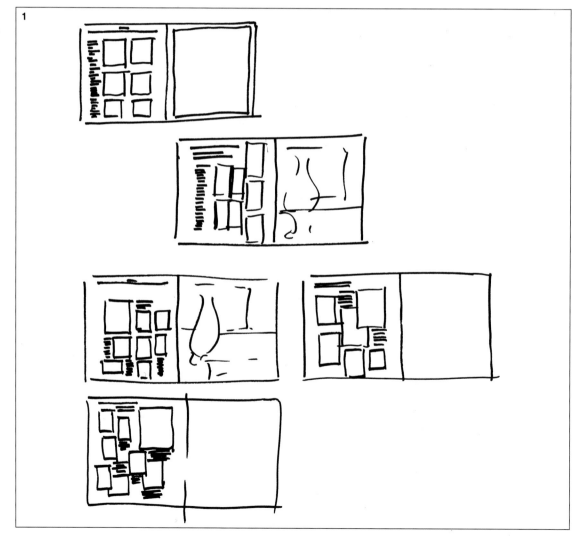

claire

2 Taking the most predominant elements, in this case the photographs, various arrangements are created. The proportions of each photograph are governed by the impression it creates on the page. These images are viewed as shapes within shapes and are blown up and reduced to be cropped and pasted up in chosen positions.

The quality of the photographs is unimportant at this layout stage and they are merely moved around to find the best arrangement. The two alternative spreads shown here indicate the evolving design process. The typography is selected from the *Marie Claire* house style and here is simply used as a visual guide.

Evening Stars

For nostalgic indulgence in nights past.
1. Period dressing, complete with tassel and lace bag, long beads and velvet-trimmed topper by Ally Capellino. 2. Versace's silk-satin dressing-gown graces more than the bedroom with an easy elegance and sensual fluidity. 3. Winter chiffon reveals all beneath a luxurious sweeping dusky grey velvet coat by Montana. 4. At Chloe the tuxedo is re-tailored; front and sleeves curve away, while satin lapels reflect long shimmering ropes of jet

5. John Galliano takes a flight of fancy: a feathered top worn with suede shorts. 6. A beaded and fringed shawl by Sara Sturgeon enhances a simple evening dress. 7. A satin sheath femme fatale-style has a chiffon scarf twined over the shoulders by Chloe. 8. Callaghan shows long, multi-stranded ropes of twinkling beads and elaborate silver clasps over a voluminous full-length evening coat

Right: beaded satin evening bag, £9.99, Next Directory No M33049; jet and bead pendant, £65, large silver and tasselled pendant, £76, jet faceted clip-on earrings, £52, all Pellini; marcasite earrings, £27.50, brooches, from a selection, Whitehill Ltd; beaded-evening shoes, £185, to order from Rayne; jet-bead necklace, £109, L'Or Noir; feather boa, £31, Dickins & Jones; beaded-edge scarf, £58, Nicole Farhi. See page 198 for stockist details

122

3

3 Using the chosen layout's typesetting specification, spaces between rules and pictures, rule widths and general instructions are indicated so that artwork can begin. The production team follows the instructions on the rough, using the pictures as position guides for the final print. These photographs, supplied as color slides, are laid out to correspond with the designer's rough. The printer returns the layout in the form of a colorproof. This is then evaluated for errors and the designer is able to make final color corrections by giving precise specifications to the printer.

4 The page emerges, with the corrections to color made. This final image concludes a process that is undertaken for each of the pages in this and every publication.

4

Evening Stars

For nostalgic indulgence in nights past. 1. Period dressing, complete with tassel and lace bag, long beads and velvet-trimmed topper by Ally Capellino. 2. Versace's silk-satin dressing-gown graces more than the bedroom with an easy elegance and sensual fluidity. 3. Winter chiffon reveals all beneath a luxurious sweeping dusky grey velvet coat by Montana. 4. At Chloé the tuxedo is re-tailored: front and sleeves curve away, while satin lapels reflect long shimmering ropes of jet

5. John Galliano takes a flight of fancy: a feathered top worn with suede shorts. 6. A beaded and fringed shawl by Sara Sturgeon enhances a simple evening dress. 7. A satin sheath femme fatale-style has a chiffon scarf twined over the shoulders by Chloé. 8. Callaghan shows long, multi-stranded ropes of twinkling beads and elaborate silver clasps over a voluminous full-length evening coat

Right: beaded satin evening bag, £9.99, Next Directory, No. M33049; jet and bead pendant, £65, large silver and tasselled pendant, £76, jet faceted clip-on earrings, £52, all Pellini; marcasite earrings, £27.50, brooches, from a selection (all in glass container), all Brats; silver pencil, from a selection, Whitehill Ltd; beaded evening shoes, £185, to order from Rayne; jet-bead necklace, £109, L'Or Noir; feather boa, £31, Dickins & Jones; beaded-edge scarf, £58, Nicole Farhi. See page 198 for stockist details

1 Research showed that teenage audiences are interested in styles and fashions rather than the fruity content of this new product. This provided the designer with an opportunity to create a distinctive brand with exciting and novel graphics. The first concepts tried out the names Mondo and Boxer, which were applied in a graphic form.

1

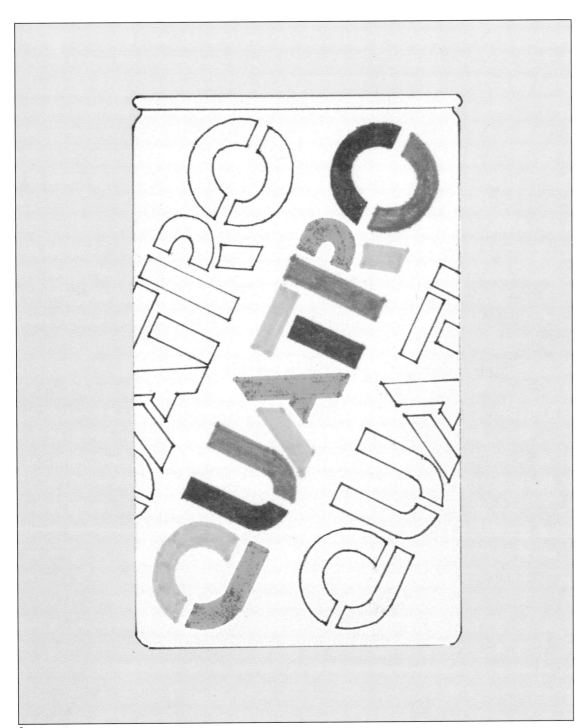

2 Eventually, the name Quatro came into being. This was a stylish yet logical choice, as the word refers to the four fruit ingredients of the product: orange, lime, lemon and cherry.

2

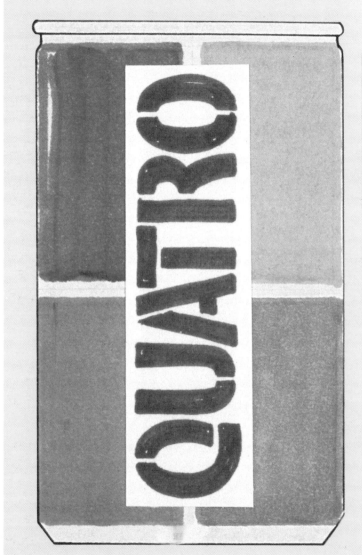

3 The next stage of development took account of the colors that represented the ingredients. Green was chosen to symbolize freshness and create immediate shelf impact. The other colors gave the product a bright, compelling appearance.

4 Further experimentation brought about the combination of the "Q" symbol and the four colors. This consolidated the major selling points of the product and formed the foundation for the design of the finished product.

5

5 The final presentation displayed the Quatro concept as a highly finished image. Pure graphics were used to create a strikingly different corporate image that stood out from the competition in a stylish and modern way.

6 The display potential of the product was realized through the bright and colorful design, which gave the product the overall appearance of a modern Pop Art image.

7 The Quatro concept was then applied to the range of packaging formats in which the product was sold. The green was again a strong feature in the bottles.

Youth Market: Case Studies

These two case studies represent completely different areas of the market. The first, designed by Mervyn Kurlansky of Pentagram, solves the problem of communicating a product to a young Japanese audience. Mervyn was asked to look at the way competitive cosmetic products for both young women and young men were being marketed and then establish an identity for a new product line and to explore a new and exciting packaging concept.

The research that was undertaken to discover a new and unique branding demanded that Mervyn understood the current trends and fashions of 18-25-year-old Japanese. Although there were reservations about the name of this new product range, "Trendy" was unanimously selected by the manufacturers because it is an internationally understood word and concept. Despite the differences between Japanese and Western languages, the word "Trendy" has a unique appeal to its target audience because of its Western connections. Pentagram was asked to design every facet of this product from the container shape and size through to its graphic presentation.

The second case study features the work of Jeri Heiden, Vice-President and Chief Art Director of Warner Brothers. Her album cover for Madonna's *True Blue* album underwent a fascinating number of technically manipulated stages as well as highly finished presentations before a final cover design was accepted. When working with this caliber of entertainer, a high priority is placed on the performer's public image and therefore the decision depends upon his or her cooperation and approval. Here is a unique opportunity to view the rejected images and get an idea of the reasons why they were not used.

1 "Trendy" cosmetics for the young. The name, selected from a huge variety of suggestions, established many factors about the product, its target and to some extent the approach to its design.

1

2

3

4

2 Having established a product name, it was important to look at its marketplace and its visual competition. Naturally, this new product needed to be sufficiently different in style and distinctive in appearance to stand out on a crowded shelf.

3 Although fashions in Japan vary widely, from the smart and conventional to the casually individual, it was discovered that young Japanese have preferences in common about cosmetics. The fashionable rivalry associated with young people in the West is not as pronounced among the young Japanese consumers.

4 It is not possible to create new images in isolation. To understand what influenced the young Japanese, it was important to seek out the way in which art in its dominant form was being applied in the environment. A realization of the importance of new architecture inspired the initial thinking.

5

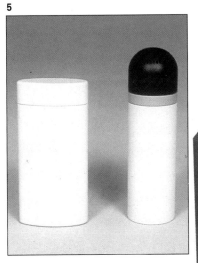

6

5

5 The first major problem was finding a container that had its own distinctive appearance. A popular activity in Japan is miming to contemporary music in bars. It is no coincidence that one of these designs resembles a modern microphone.

6 As the container developed, thoughts turned to the post-modernist architecture of Japan. The container required a distinctive quality that would appeal to the young. Color and decorative additions were applied to build its visual character.

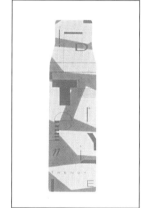

8 As the design develops the architecture theme becomes clear, although the design now seems too smart and passive.

7 The early graphics for the container explored the shape through typographic image and popular illustrative ideas. The typography designs looked at the characteristics of Japanese letterforms and reconstructed them in a visual pattern that expressed the product name. The images were both functional and decorative in style and different from the products of the competition. The designer could be confident that this sort of imagery would appeal to a youth market as it appears frequently in modern magazines.

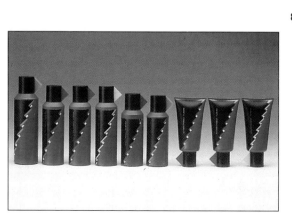

8

9 The distinctive shapes and this classic form created by the profiles of modern Japanese fashions permeated the images as they emerged.

10 The colors and shape of this design were deliberately formulated to highlight the inherent qualities of current Japanese high fashion.

11 The earlier typographic styling is resurrected in these examples. The letterforms are broken down into abstract shapes and an impression emerges of Western calligraphy.

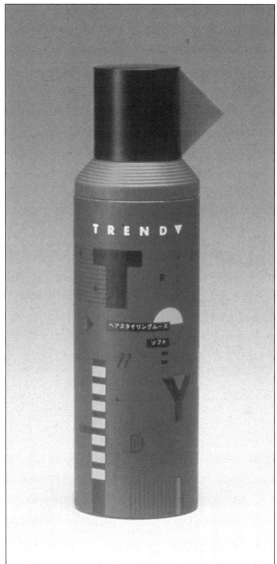

12 This final design retains the best features of the previous designs, from the package design to the surface graphics. After some consideration of potential production problems, it was decided to use the straight cap with the colored tab. This naturally influenced the rest of the design and it was decided to go ahead with the lively and animated graphics that we see here. The design is also functional in terms of product identification, as it was possible to color-code the product range. The distinctive cap device helped to identify the soft packs (the tubes of cosmetics) with the rest of the family of products.

13 The container's surface graphics became a dazzling device used in the advertising, with brand awareness reinforced by specific use of the "T" of Trendy.

13

1 *True Blue*, album by Madonna. The first task in a project of this scale was to liaise with the photographer, in this case Herb Ritts, to establish some design formulae and visual approaches before calling in and arranging appointments with Madonna. At the first photo session, some exploratory images (mainly in black and white) of strikingly different formats were shot. The underlying theme decided on for this project was the mystical beauty of Madonna in a retrospective context. It was felt that black and white photography would give the project a base on which to model a style.

2 A selection was made from the black and white photographs. Then composites were assembled using different typefaces and layout designs. The art director now wanted to experiment with color, and some hand-tinted, blue-toned bromides were produced. These were softer than pure black and white and gave a more period-like quality. The type styles selected were distinctive.

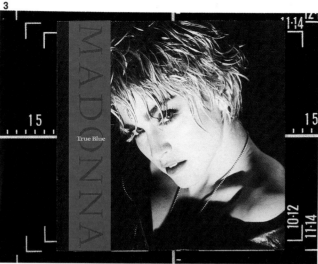

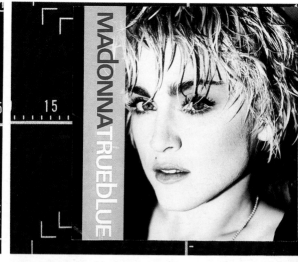

.3 To contrast with the layout of the first composites, further designs were produced to give a more teasing and rakish quality to the image of the star. A reduced-strength tint band is strung across the design to emphasize the type. Again, the typography and color were used to give a softer quality against the stark, contrasty black and white photography.

4 A close-up image has been severely cropped to emphasize the Madonna stare. This made an attractive composition and a natural space appeared in which to apply a hint of color to the otherwise black and white surface.

5 All the previous images were rejected by the performer. A black and white photograph was selected and a hand-tinted version was created to resemble a Technicolor film of the 1950s. An inexpensive color print was made solely for the designer to produce a mock-up, but it was this poor-quality color print that was finally used as artwork because Madonna particularly liked its pale, soft, washed-out colors. This is the final version used in the U.S. where there was no typography applied to the cover itself, as this information was carried on a separate sticker.

6 The final international cover incorporates the bold strip of type with the soft 1950s Technicolor tints to the photograph giving the overall image a nostalgic beauty. A solid blue, which complements the colors of the photograph, has been applied to the back cover with the word "Madonna" picked out in silver. The hand script of the body matter has become a classic style for pop album covers and gives a sophisticated feel.

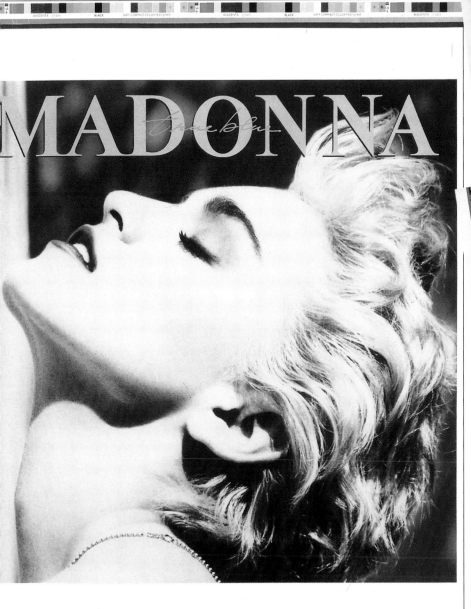

7

7 The less expensively produced covers for the single and the "maxi" have a closer relationship to the early composites than does the final front of the album cover.

Sophisticated Market: Case Studies

This area of graphic design pays particular attention to a well-defined sector of the market. The following case studies have been selected because they communicate quality of service or product to a sophisticated audience. Designing for such a market demands an understanding of its lifestyle, income and cultural perception, all of which govern the choice of image.

The first case study explores the decisions involved in the creation of a company's annual report. The company, with its range of activities in communications and publishing, required a quality image to enhance its financial statements. The visual approach demanded a positive presentation of the group's commercial achievements. The brief from the chairman of Quarto was precise and succinct: "Create an annual report that reflects the successful growth of a rapidly developing group involved in publishing, photography, design and printing." The first part of the report was to be a clear visual and verbal description of the dynamic success of the company's activities, followed by a financial report that confirmed to the shareholders that the company's financial performance was as impressive as its creative business activities.

The subject of the second case study is very different from the company report, although the target audience is equally discerning. This design, for the launch of Ashbys new Premier Ground Coffee line, reflects the product's exclusivity. Ashbys experience in the coffee market dates from 1850, and the company is considered one of Europe's most experienced and respected specialist importers.

The brief to the designers was to create an image for a premier specialist brand of coffee, aimed at the connoisseur. The target market was experienced ground-coffee drinkers who were adventurous in their choice of coffee, and keen to try new brands. The countries of origin of the coffee were Brazil, Kenya and Colombia, and this exotic choice was aimed specifically at the luxury end of the market. To guarantee the coffee's freshness and purity, in keeping with Ashby's high standards, a foil-laminated pack was used with an innovative valve on the back to allow the coffee to breathe, so that it reached the consumer in the best condition. To retain the authentic nature of this product while projecting an image of superior quality, the designer chose to use rich colors and evocative illustration.

1 The first task in the creation of Quarto's annual report was to decide how the information was to be displayed. It seemed logical to subdivide the company's activities into manageable sections. A plan of these sections was outlined under topic headings, with a list of pictures that would depict them graphically. It seemed appropriate to devote the front of the report to colorful graphics, leaving the technical and financial section to follow.

2

and possessed the right degree of sophistication, and also looked businesslike and practical. These thumbnail sketches reveal early thinking on layout formulae, grids and the positioning of illustrations.

QUARTO   4TO   folding & twice
4to

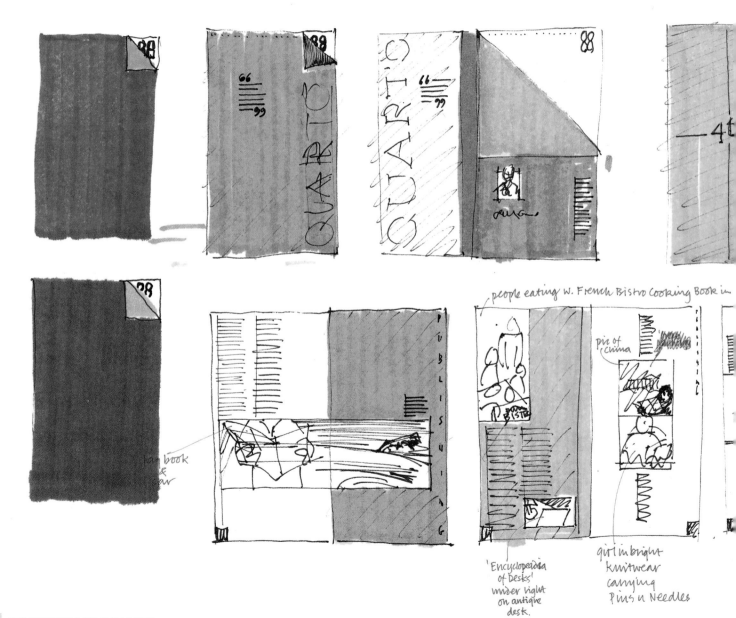

QUARTO

QUARTO

4to

PUBLISHING

fun book & ear

people eating w. French Bistro Cooking Book in

pic of china

'Encyclopedia of Desks' under light on antique desk.

girl in bright knitwear carrying Pins n Needles

‍PORATE BROCHURE

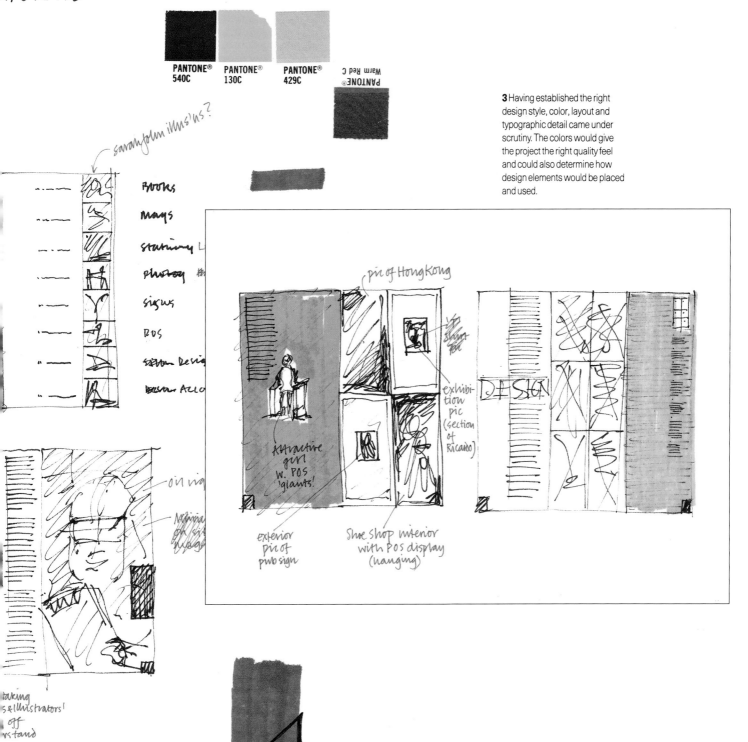

PANTONE® 540C
PANTONE® 130C
PANTONE® 429C
PANTONE® Warm Red C

3 Having established the right design style, color, layout and typographic detail came under scrutiny. The colors would give the project the right quality feel and could also determine how design elements would be placed and used.

sarah john illus'ns?

BOOKS

mags

stationy

photog

signs

POS

screen design

brochur A4 C

BOOKS

pic of Hong Kong

exhibition pic (section of Ricardo)

DESIGN

Attractive girl W. POS 'giants!'

exterior pic of pub sign

Shoe shop interior with POS display (hanging)

taking
s & Illustrators!
off
stand

SOPHISTICATED MARKET   125

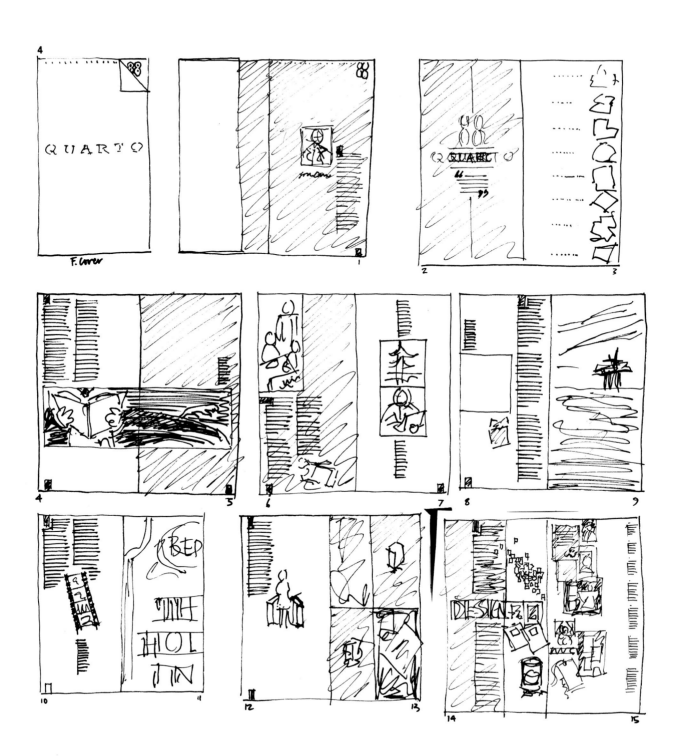

5

4 The pages could be subdivided to pinpoint the activities of the business by means of selected photographic images and illustrations, along with typographic layout. Once the pages had been made to follow this coordinated plan, the design team discussed the next stage. The design so far had been shaped for in-house discussion between designers and so only a rough layout was required.

5 Having established the format of the presentation, closer attention was now paid to the space and typographic detail. As the design relied on precise use of space, the type image needed to communicate the qualities and sophistication of the service and products. Even the choice of papers on which the images appeared had to be arty yet businesslike.

6

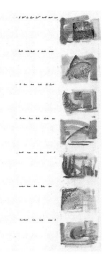

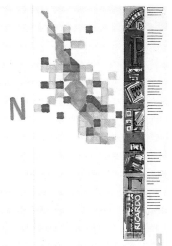

DESIGN

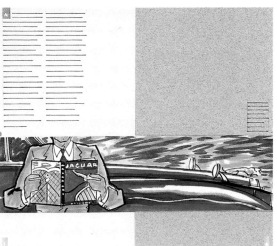

6 Everything was now prepared for the final stage in the design, in which a visualizer was called in to be briefed on the client presentation. Paper quality, image, and typographic layout would still only need to be indicated as a visual, but it would still be necessary to communicate the final appearance of the annual report to the client.

7 The next stage, following the client's approval of the visual, was to produce and collate all the elements. The text was written by the copywriter and submitted in draft form for amendment and approval. It was then cast off and typefaces were selected. Visual components were added and colored tints considered. Meanwhile, photographs were selected from a picture library and other photographs and illustrations were commissioned, and the final images were selected for the pages. The financial and technical section was collated, and the typographical style that had been established in the early part was carried through.

The Quarto Group is a uniqu of successful companies specialising in book package publishing, magazine publis photography, silk-screen p creative design.

7

In thirteen years, the accelerated to the fore

Today ha

8 Pages were finally assembled and artworked, with specific color choices indicated. A proof was then created for the client to assess. The financial section was left until the end and set up as the last item for the client to check once final performance figures were available.

9 Because of the legal requirements governing annual reports, a very strict schedule for printing was adhered to. Color proofs were quickly despatched to both client and designer for checking. The job was carried out to coincide with the production of the shareholders' voting and proxy forms, with all of the material despatched as an end-of-year information pack.

1

2

1 The concept for this product was inspired by its exotic origins. The first design used commissioned illustrations that identified the distinctive nature of each of the countries in which the coffee grows. To enhance the impression of pure, natural quality, earthy colors were used, and these formed the basis of a superior-looking image. At this stage the branding lacked an identity, and so this early design relied on the name of the holding company, Paulig.

2 To emphasize the product's traditions and the company's history, the name Ashbys was highlighted, the name connoting the quality attained during almost 150 years in the market. It also gave a familiar, easy-to-remember ring to the product. The colors chosen for the visuals, now an important factor in individualizing each product in the line, were deep blue for Kenyan coffee, burgundy for Colombian and bottle green for Brazilian. Illustrations were created in a popular style that identified each country by means of its costumes.

3 The final product retains all the basic design qualities of the visuals, while emphasizing the importance of the name and adding the company's historical credentials. The colors relate closely to the visuals, with the exception of the red pack, which has become much brighter, enhancing visual impact. In their final form the illustrations have become more figurative and give an impression of the scenery of each of the countries.

Special Market: Case Study

THERE WILL BE occasions when a graphic design project is targeted at a special audience. This audience has very specific needs, tastes or aspirations and the intention in these cases is to focus on the specific requirements and to present the information in a sympathetic format and style.

A wide range of projects comes into this category. They could include an invitation to an open air festival, a group wanting special medical advice or advice or products aimed at individual professional groups. When investigating the initial stages of your special project, it will be vital for you to gain some knowledge and understanding of the people with whom you wish to communicate.

The special market case study shown in the following pages documents the gradual build-up campaign to promote newly-built office premises situated in the heart of London's Soho district. This exclusive development, commanding some of the highest rents for office accommodation in the city,

required a special approach in its appeal to potential clients. The brief simply instructed the designer to produce a promotion that reflected the prestigious environment and that was sufficiently international in its visual approach to encourage overseas clients to reserve offices within the development.

In preparing this work the designer had to bear in mind the range of materials the design would be applied to. The designer had to concern himself with the initial corporate identity, which would communicate a visual theme for this development. The visual theme would then be carried through on the printed stationery, on advertisements and special invitation packages and on the banners and bunting which heralded the launch of the development.

1 The first stage of this project was to develop a distinguishable identity to give a recognizable image to all aspects of the forthcoming promotion. The initial thumbnail sketches exploit the use of the number 20, adopting an old-fashioned style to blend with the development's locality.

1

2

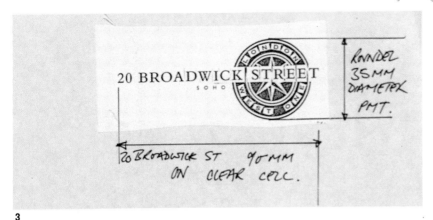

2 It was decided to develop two basic themes: one which retained the historical feeling and another that reflected the modern and contemporary appeal of this new building. Rough visuals were first created and worked up as a presentation to show the developers.

3 The client chose the more modern design and the final stage was to create artwork which would be used and printed in different applications. The design now incorporated a compass, a device to get across its central location in the heart of London's West End.

3

4

4 The first application of this image was a foil-embossed logo applied to a loose-leaf folder. The folder contained the printed specifications of the development and, for an initial response, these were mailed to a list of prospective clients.

4

5

20 BROADWICK STREET

GENERAL SPECIFICATION

DESCRIPTION

The eight storey building provides offices on the first to fifth floors, two residential units on the sixth floor, reception at ground floor level together with car parking, ancillary offices and storage at basement level. A retail/showroom unit fronting Broadwick Street is also available. Air conditioning plant, water storage and lift motors are located at roof level.

2.   STRUCTURE

3.   EXTERNAL ELEVATIONS

a.   Broadwick Street and Berwick Street Facades

These elevations are designed on the concept of the "rainscreen". The main envelope is formed of double glazed thermally broken aluminium window frames and heavily insulated cladding panels of composite steel and polystyrene construction supported on extruded aluminium cladding rails. On the outside face aluminium panels finished in three shades of textured metallic paint provide a very high quality finish and conceal fan coil units recessed into the external wall beneath window cills. On the recessed Broadwick Street elevation electrically operated external venetian blinds withdraw behind the outer panels at window heads.

Over two thirds of the width of the Broadwick Street facade a shallow projecting bay provides increased internal floor area and architectural modelling. On both street facades the upper storeys are set back to comply with Town Planning requirements.

The lower part of the street elevations from pavement level to the cill of the first floor windows is clad in a flame textured Sardinian Beige granite. Shop fronts are aluminium framed with a paint finish matching the aluminium panels on the elevation above.

b.   Rear Elevation

On the rear elevations the external wall is formed of windows and cladding panels similar to the street elevations but the aluminium rainscreen panels are omitted. The external face is finished in a PVF2 paint finish with panel joints sealed with recessed neoprene gaskets.

4.   INTERNAL FINISHES

a.   Entrance Hall

The office premises are entered via a recessed entrance beneath a projecting canopy. A curved metal glazed screen within which the entrance door is located forms a part of the perimeter of a cylindrical seating area which provides the focus of the reception area. Provision is made for the installation of an entryphone system by the occupier.

Walls of horizontal panels finished in an off white spray paint separated by recessed metallic strips are complimented by a floor of polished Sardinian Beige granite which relates to the granite finish to the street facades. Within the cylindrical seating area the ceiling is on three levels formed of concentric fibrous plaster forms with integrated feature lighting. The reception desk, which has been designed to integrate with the wall panelling, is provided with a polished granite counter. Lift doors and a door to the main stair lobby open directly off the entrance hall.

5 The specification sheets carried the project identity printed in two colors, either as letterheads, where the logo appeared in the top right-hand corner, or in an abridged version at the foot of the page.

6 At the same time that the marketing literature was being distributed, a series of press advertisements ran in a variety of newspapers and magazines, both in black and white and in color. The advertisement layouts needed to conform both to the individual printing specifications of the newspapers and magazines and to the overall campaign. The initial styling however was loose enough for variations to be created.

6

8

7 Black and white advertisements were created using reversed-out type on a solid black shape with the logo used as a sun motif, entering from the right-hand side of the design.

8 Alternative advertisements were created which pinpointed the location of the development. Spot color was used on the logo. This design retained the same style as the previous advertisement, but used white space where the other had black.

we've prepared a Communications Pack to h

guidelines and advice on

on all aspects of buil

We use the letters of our alphabet every

hase, investments or the

ease and convenient, taking them almost as much for gr

, which you can adapt to suit any

the air we breath. We do not realise that each of these

basis throughout the year. elp you

ness service today only as the result of a long and lab

on all aspects of building society

the present of evolution in

investments or the like, you

which you can adapt to suit any

9 The next item to design was the promotional brochure which was to contain twelve pages. A client presentation was produced using black and white photographs of the Soho area. These were hand-colored for the client presentation rough. The first inside spread made use of tracing paper as a device for diffusing the large text printed on the page below.

10 The front pages were used to build up a picture of the building's environment before homing in on the actual premises. The building itself was not shown until the center spread. The specifications and architect's drawings were displayed at the back of the brochure so that there was a natural progression for the reader from casual browsing to examining specific technical detail. Copy was commissioned to fit the format of the design.

SOHO – THE HEART OF WEST ONE

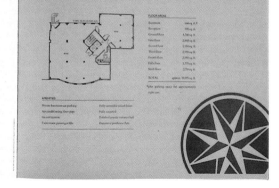

11 The finished brochure, printed in silver, blue and a hint of red, set a business-like style that reflects the overall quality of this up-scale project. A tracing paper cover is used to diffuse the first page and adds a sense of mystery and intrigue to the project.

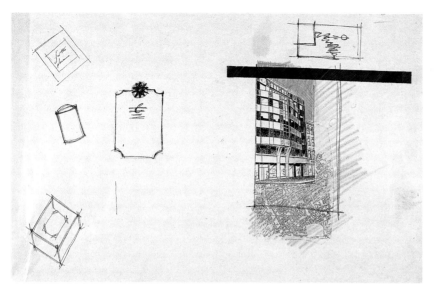

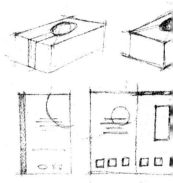

13 Ultimately the idea that was found most appealing was to present an exquisite fruit pie with the invitation, so a design evolved for this package. These early drawings formed a basis for the development of a container.

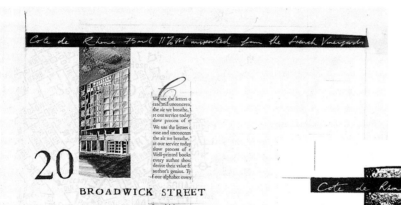

12 The next step in the project was to create a theme for the launch party. As Soho is renowned for its continental food and wine, the original concept for the invitation was to send a bottle of red wine on which the label itself was the invitation. This idea was finally rejected and a new scheme was sought.

12

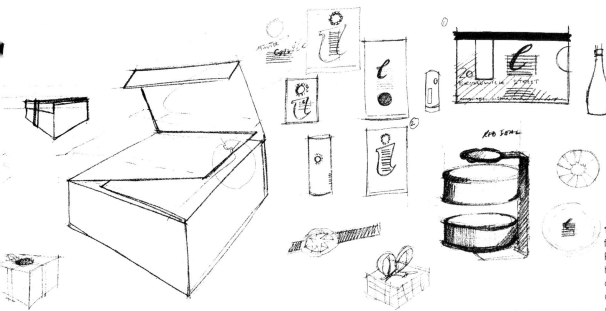

14 The final carton along with the fruit pie (created by a famous French patisserie based in the heart of Soho) made a highly original invitation. Each was delivered by messenger to potential clients.

15 The final stage in this project was to create the banners and flags used to decorate the exterior of the building for the launch.

Glossary

Artwork Any type of image that is of a high enough standard to be reproduced.

Bleed That part of an image which extends beyond the trim marks on a page.

Body text The main, straight text as distinct from headings, and the like.

Book jacket The printed sheet that wraps around the outside of a book carrying the title, author, and any other information.

Border Decorative device with many applications: commonly used at the edge of the design to frame typography.

Brief Guidelines prepared at the beginning of a project, usually drawn up by the client or project leader as technical advice for the designer, normally including financial costings.

Capitals The large, upper case letters of a typeface, as distinct from lower case letters.

Characters The word used in typography to describe letters, numerals, punctuation marks, other symbols, or space between words.

Client The person or persons commissioning or sponsoring the project.

Collage A combination of a variety of components such as cut-outs, photographs, and paint, to create a single image.

Color proof The initial printed sheets which are run off enabling the printer, artist, and client to check for registration and color before the main run.

Column An arrangement of text on lines, one above the other, with each line of roughly equal length.

Composite Sometimes called a comp. Used to describe a single image created by merging two or more transparencies. Also used for a presentation assembled from the graphic elements which resembles the finished print.

Composition The arrangement of the graphic design elements within the design area.

Concept The idea underlying a graphic design brief. This will arise either from the client direct or out of meetings to discuss the project.

Copywriter A writer whose work is specifically aimed at the promotion of products or services and which appears in advertisements, brochures, catalogues, etc.

Cropping Ls L-shaped, interlocking pieces of paper or cardboard used by designers to place over photographs or transparencies to help in the decision-making process. The Ls act as a framing device, so that the designer can decide how to trim the illustrative matter.

Cyan The standardized shade of blue ink used in the four-color process.

Dummy pack A prototype that shows how a three-dimensional object, such as a book or package, will look by using the proposed materials but not necessarily showing all the graphics.

Four-color process The process of reproducing full color by separating the image into three printing primary colors – cyan, magenta, and yellow – plus black. Each of the four colors is carried on a separate plate, which, when printed over each other, reproduces the effect of all the colors in the original.

Galleys The columns of text that are produced uncut from the typesetting machinery. These are used both for proof checking and making up layouts.

Gradation Blending of tones together in such a way as to make the tone change almost imperceptibly.

Grids The sheets used in design to represent a spread or design area on which all the relevant measurements - page size, margins, trim marks, and so on – are printed. This enables the designer to place all the components accurately.

Hand lettering The technique of constructing letters with artificial aids and accurate measurements.

Illustration The term used to describe an image that has been drawn as distinct from one that has been photographed.

Image The visual subject matter of an illustration, design, or photograph.

Justified The term used to describe lines of text that are spaced and set to align with both the left- and right-hand margins.

Letterhead Stationery that carries the name, address, telephone number, and often a logo or design, of a business or individual.

Livery Distinguishing graphics used and applied to forms of transport, uniforms etc., to represent the corporate image of the company or business. Usually an extension of the images used in the logo or stationery of the company.

Logo Initials or words cast as a single unit usually as a company signature or trademark.

Magenta The standardized shade of red ink used in the four-color process.

Market A specific audience with an acknowledged interest in a given service or product.

Masthead The title and/or logo of a magazine or newspaper as it appears on the front cover.

Medium Refers to any type of coloring agent such as ink, paint, dye etc., that is used to cover a surface.

Montage Photographs cut and organized to create a single picture.

Packaging Packs or cartons designed for individual products.

Presentation visual (or comprehensive) Any graphic material or illustrations made for the purpose of showing the client what the proposed design or finished product will look like.

Printer's proof The initial sheets printed prior to the full print run on which the printer and designer make any final adjustments.

Reverse out The term used to describe the process by which an image appears white out of a solid background. It is usually achieved by photomechanical transfer techniques.

Rough visuals Initial sketches made prior to artwork. They are not as detailed as actual finished work, but echo the visual presence of a printed piece of work.

Sans serif The term used to describe typefaces that do not have small terminal strokes on the individual letters.

Scamp sheet A sheet of thumbnail sketches that is used during the early stages of the visualization process.

Serifs The small terminating strokes on individual letters.

Spot color A special color not available in the four-color printing process, which can be added to a four-color or a black and white design.

Style A distinctive manner of presenting an image.

Subhead A heading used to break up a chapter or page in a publication.

Text The main body of words in any publication.

Thumbnail sketch A very rough, small, and quick initial sketch that is used to work out an idea.

Tint A faint color often used as a background before printing.

Tone The varying shades of a single color.

Typeface A term used to describe the whole range of lettering available in typesetting.

Typesetting The assembly of type for printing by hand, machine, or photography.

Type sheets Pre-printed sheets showing a variety of typefaces which are then used by designers for reference when choosing suitable faces.

Typography The art, general design, and appearance of printed matter using type.

Visualizer The visualizer gives visual form to an initial idea. He or she translates ideas into graphic terms.

Yellow The third color in the four-color process.

Index

Credits

Quarto would like to thank the following for their help with this publication and for permission to reproduce copyright material. Every effort has been made to trace and acknowledge all copyright holders. Quarto would like to apologize if any omissions have been made.

p9 *1* Biba. **pp10/11** Mappin & Webb, *1, 3, 4* Robert Opie, *2* By courtesy of the Board of Trustees of the Victoria and Albert Museum. **pp12/13** *1* By courtesy of the Board of Trustees of the Victoria and Albert Museum, *3* Cassandre, *4* Robert Opie. **pp14/15** *1, 2, 4* By courtesy of the Board of Trustees of the Victoria and Albert Museum. **pp16/17** *1* Alan Swann, *2, 3, 4, 6* Pentagram, *5* Conran. **pp18/19** Duffy Design. **pp20/21** *4* Michael Thierens, Duffy Design, Michael Manwaring, Conran, Fortnum & Mason. **pp22/23** *3* David Davies Associates. **pp24/25** *2* Pentagram U.S.A. **pp26/27** *2* David Quay/Letraset, *3* Michael Doret. **pp28/29** *1* Pat Schleger, *3* Smith & Milton, *4* Duffy Design. **pp30/31** *1* Duffy Design, *2* Pentagram, *3* Fitch & Co., *4* Alan Chan Design Co. Hong Kong. **pp32/33** *6* Alan Swann *7, 8* David Davies Associates. **pp34/35** *1* Pentagram, *2* Fitch & Co., *3* Buro Rolf Muller. **pp36/37** *2, 3* Buro Rolf Muller. **pp38/39** *1* Alan Swann, *2* GGK Basel, *3* GFTGB, *4* Borders, Perrin & Norrander. **pp40/41** *1* Artwork, B. & M. Unterweger, *2* Michael Brock, *3* DMB & B, *4* Bagby Design. **pp42/43** *1* Carter Wong, *2* Malcolm Southwood Associates, *3* Robert Valentine Inc. U.S.A., *4* Heller Breene. **pp44/45** *4* Bagby Design, *5, 6* Coley Porter Bell. **pp46/47** *4* Banks & Miles, *5, 6* Conran. **pp48/49** *3, 4, 5* Ian Logan, *6* Immagine Design, *7* Crabtree & Evelyn. **p50** *top left* Duffy Design, *bottom left* Pentagram **p51** *top left* Pentagram *bottom left* Duffy Design. **pp52/53** Quaker Oats Company *1–5* Lewis Moberley, Duffy Design. **pp54/55** *1* Lewis Moberley, *2* Ian Logan. **pp56/57** *1* Pentagram, *2* Ziggurat. **pp58/59** *1* Barry Tucker Design, *2* Howard Brown, *3* Ian Logan, *4* Ziggurat. **pp60/61** *1* Duffy Design, *2* Carin Goldberg. **pp62/63** *1* Lloyd Northover, *2, 3* Barrie Tucker. **pp64/65** *1* Smith & Milton, *2, 3* Michael Peters. **pp66/67** *1, 2* Warner Books, *3* Nettle Design Ltd., *4, 7* Ziggurat, *5* WBMG Inc., *6* Trickett & Webb. **pp68/69** Duffy Design, *1* Gariboldi, Parisi, Verga, *2* Next. **pp70/71** *1, 2* Carin Goldberg, *3* Michael Mabry. **pp72/73** *1* Pentagram U.S.A., *2* David Davies Associates. **pp74/75** *1* Fortnum & Mason, *2, 3, 4* Michael Peters, *5* David Davies Associates, *6* Ian Logan. **pp78/79** *1* Fitch & Co., *2* Carter Wong. **pp80/81** *1, 3* The Face, *2* Blitz, *4* GFTGB. **pp82/83** *1* Michael Peters, *2* Conran, *3* Art-work, *4* Emigre, *5* Bagby Design. **pp84/85** *2* Jones & Co. **pp86/87** *1* Minale, Tattersfield & Partners, *2* Cyb Design Consultants Ltd. **pp88/89** *1, 2* Michael Peters. **pp90/91** *1* Carter Wong, *2, 5* Fitch & Co., *3* Michael Peters, *4* Cyb Design. **pp96–101** Michael Peters. **pp102–105** Marie Claire. **pp106–111** Michael Peters. **p112–117** Pentagram. **pp118–121** Warner Bros. Records Inc. **pp122–129** Bridgewater Design. **pp130/131** Michael Peters. **pp132–139** Grey Matter Design.